Sonia Gallico

guide to the excavations of OSTIA
ANTICA
with a section about the Renaissance Borgo

ATS ITALIA EDITRICE

Theatrical Mask (proscenium of the Theatre)

INTRODUCTION

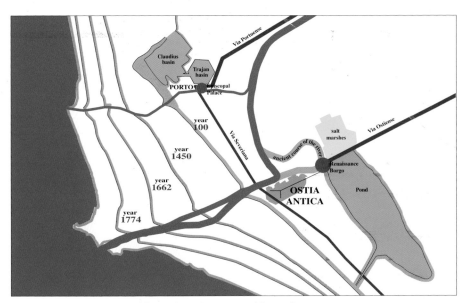

The seashore in Roman times and following forward movements of the coastline

T HE ANCIENT ROMAN TOWN OF OSTIA (FROM LATIN "OSTIUM": MOUTH), TOUCH-
ED BY THE RIVER AND THE SEA AS WELL, WAS SITUATED IN AN AREA QUITE DIFFERENT
FROM WHAT IT IS NOW. IT WAS CHARACTERISED BY VARIOUS ELEMENTS, TODAY NO LONGER
EXISTING OR CHANGED:
- A COASTLINE BACK OF ABOUT 4 KM (THE EXTENSION OF THE SHORELINE SEAWARDS IS DUE TO
THE ALLUVIUM DEPOSITED AND COMPACTED BY THE RIVER THROUGH THE CENTURIES);
- A VERY BIG BEND OF THE MAIN BRANCH OF THE TIBER, ERASED SUDDENLY IN NOVEMBER 1557,
AT NIGHT, WHEN THE RIVER CHANGED ITS COURSE DURING A FLOOD;
- A NO LONGER EXISTING POND (JUST A LIGHT DEPRESSION STILL SURVIVED ON THE GROUND)
WHICH WAS LINKED TO THE SEA BY A CANAL;
- THE PRESENCE OF SALT MARSHES EXTENDING BETWEEN THE RIVER AND THE POND. KNOWN
SINCE THE ETRUSCAN TIME, THESE WERE AN IMPORTANT INCOME, BECAUSE SALT WAS AN
ESSENTIAL INGREDIENT FOR FOOD PRESERVATION.
OSTIA WAS NOT AN ISOLATED TOWN. IN FACT ALONG THE ROAD WHICH LINKED IT TO ROME,
THE VIA OSTIENSE, TOWARDS THE TIBER, MANY FARMS WERE BUILT, SOME OF THEM CONSIDER-
ED PROPER RUSTIC VILLAS. THEN, SINCE THE III CENTURY AD, THE VIA SEVERIANA CONNECT-
ED THE TOWN WITH THE SURROUNDING AREAS, TOWARDS THE SEA; ON THE NORTH THERE WAS
THE TOWN OF PORTO (BUILT SINCE THE I C. AD) AND ITS NECROPOLIS, WHILE IN THE
SOUTH THE COAST WAS SPOTTED WITH NUMEROUS AND IMPORTANT SUMMER RESIDENCES,
OVERLOOKING THE SEA.
NOW A WIDE ARCHAEOLOGICAL - NATURALISTIC PARK IS BEING STUDIED WHICH SHOULD
INCLUDE ALL THOSE PRE-EXISTING AREAS LINKED BY ONE SINGLE ROUTE.

THE ORIGINS OF OSTIA

T HE ORIGINS OF OSTIA ARE STILL QUITE UNKNOWN, EVEN THOUGH MANY STUDIES HAVE BEEN CARRIED OUT. THE ROMAN POET ENNIUS (239-169 BC) WRITES: "AFTER THE SUCCESSION TO THE THRONE OF ANCUS MARTIUS, OSTIA WAS FOUNDED, WHERE THE TIBER FLOWS INTO THE SALTISH SEA (ANNALES II, 84-86). ALSO THE HISTORIAN LIVY (59 BC - 17 AD) ATTRIBUTES THE FOUNDATION OF THE TOWN TO THE FORTH KING OF ROME, ANCUS MARTIUS, WHO LIVED, ACCORDING TO TRADITION, IN THE SECOND HALF OF THE 7TH CENTURY BC: "THE TOWN AND ITS SURROUNDING AREAS DEVELOPED UNDER THIS KING: (...) THE ROMAN DOMINION EXTENDED TO THE SEA" AND, ON THE MOUTH OF THE TIBER, THE TOWN OF OSTIA WAS FOUNDED; SOME SALT MARSHES WERE SET UP NEARBY" (HISTORIAE I, 33,9). NO TRACES HAVE BEEN FOUND OF THE TOWN IN THE KINGS' AGE. SOME HISTORIANS EVEN DOUBT ITS EXISTENCE; OTHERS THINK IT WAS BELOW THE EXISTING TOWN. THE HYPOTHESIS OF PROFESSOR BARBIERI IS INTERESTING: HE THINKS THAT IN KINGS' AGE OSTIA OVERLOOKED THE NORTHERN BANK OF THE POND, NEAR THE SALT MARSHES.

THE REPUBLICAN TOWN

T HE MOST ANCIENT REMAINS OF OSTIA DATE FROM THE SECOND HALF OF THE 4TH C. BC, WHEN ROME HAD ALREADY DEFEATED THE ETRUSCANS, AND ITS DOMINIONS EXTENDED FROM THE SOUTHERN BORDER OF TUSCANY AND THAT OF LATIUM. THE WALLS OF THE NEW TOWN AT THE MOUTH OF THE TIBER DATE BACK TO ABOUT 330-320 BC AND WERE BUILT IN "OPUS QUADRATUM".

IT WAS A "CASTRUM", A TYPICAL FORTIFIED PLACE, BUILT MOST LIKELY TO DEFEND THE RIVER ENTRANCE TO ROME. THE DEFENSIVE WALLS FORMED A RECTANGLE, WITH THE LONGER SIDE PARALLEL TO THE RIVER AND MEASURED 194 X 126 M.; THEY WERE BUILT WITH LARGE TUFA BLOCKS FROM FIDENE (A PLACE ON THE TIBER, TO THE NORTH OF ROME, NOW NEAR THE RACCORDO ANULARE). INSIDE THERE WAS A CARDO AND A DECUMANUS WHICH FORMED A FORUM, A SQUARE, AT THEIR JUNCTION: THIS KIND OF STRUCTURE WILL BE USED ALSO IN THE FORTHCOMING URBAN EXPANSION. WE HAVE NO HISTORICAL SOURCES OF THIS OSTIA, WHICH BECAME IMPORTANT IN THE III C. BC, WHEN ROME CAME INTO CONTACT WITH THE TOWNS OF THE MAGNA GRECIA -

Castrum walls

AMONG THEM, TARANTO (CONQUERED IN 272 BC); IN THE SAME PERIOD OSTIA STARTED ITS HEGEMONY ON SOUTHERN ITALY, FORESHADOWING THE FUTURE CONFLICT WITH CARTHAGE. THE FIRST NEWS ABOUT OSTIA DATES EXACTLY FROM THE III C. BC:

- IN 267 BC FOUR "QUAESTORES CLASSICI" (FROM LATIN "CLASSIS" = FLEET, THEY WERE THE MAGISTRATES IN CHARGE OF IT) WERE APPOINTED IN ROME AND THE "PROVINCIA QUAESTORIA OSTIENSIS" WAS ORGANISED. SINCE THEN, ONE OF THE QUAESTORS LIVED PERMANENTLY IN OSTIA - THIS IS EVIDENCE OF THE STRATEGIC IMPORTANCE OF THE TOWN.

- IN 217 BC, ACCORDING TO THE HISTORIAN LIVY, SOME SHIPS LEFT FROM HERE IN ORDER TO SUPPLY THE ROMAN ARMY OF FOOD. THE ROMANS WERE FIGHTING IN SPAIN AGAINST THE CARTHAGINIANS LED BY HANNIBALIS WHO HAD CONQUERED THE TOWN OF SAGUNTO.

- IN 211 BC PUBLIO CORNELIUS SCIPIO SAILED FROM OSTIA TO SPAIN, WHERE HE DEFEATED THE CARTHAGINIAN ARMY THREE TIMES DURING THE SECOND PUNIC WAR, BETWEEN 209 AND 208.

WHAT WE KNOW ABOUT OSTIA DURING THE II AND I C. BC IS NOT MUCH AND FRAGMENTARY, EVEN THOUGH THE TOWN HAD SURELY A GREAT BUILDING DEVELOPMENT OUT OF THE CASTRUM.

IN 87 BC, DURING THE CIVIL WARS WHICH DEVASTATED ROME, MARIUS, LEADER OF THE POPULAR PARTY, SEIZED OSTIA, AS SOME SOLDIERS OF HIS BITTER RIVAL SULLA, LEADER OF THE HOLIGARCHIC PARTY, ESCAPED THERE. VERY SOON SULLA RECONQUERED AND SACKED THE TOWN.

IN 80 BC, THE "SULLAN WALLS" WERE BUILT AROUND AN AREA OF 69 HECTARES AND, IN THE MIDDLE OF THE FIRST CENTURY A TEMPLE WAS REALISED IN THE AREA OF THE FORUM. IN 67 BC, THE ROMAN FLEET WAS ATTACKED BY PIRATES FROM CILICIA (A REGION IN TURKEY). THIS IS THE LAST NEWS BEFORE THE REIGN OF AUGUSTUS.

THE IMPERIAL ERA

UNDER THE EMPEROR AUGUSTUS (27 BC - 14 AD), OSTIA BEGAN TO BE RENOVATED IN ITS MONUMENTAL AND BUILDING PARTS. ALTHOUGH MANY BUILDINGS OF THIS PERIOD HAVE BEEN RECONSTRUCTED LATER, THE THEATRE AND THE PIAZZALE DELLE CORPORAZIONI DATE FROM THE AUGUSTAN AGE. UNDER HIS SON TIBERIUS (14-37), THE FORUM WITH THE TEMPLE DEDICATED TO ROME AND AUGUSTUS WAS BUILT. IN THE MIDDLE OF THE I CENTURY, OSTIA REACHED A REMARKABLE DEVELOPMENT ALSO IN THE HARBOUR ACTIVITIES BUT, DUE TO THE SHALLOW WATER, THE BIG BOATS HAD TO MOOR OUT AT SEA AND LIGHTER THE GOODS. IT WAS PERHAPS FOR THIS REASON THAT THE EMPEROR CLAUDIUS (41-54) DECIDED TO HAVE A NEW PORT BUILT 3 KM TO THE NORTH OF OSTIA, ALTHOUGH THE EXPERTS DID NOT AGREE WITH HIS DECISION, THUS STARTING THE NEW SETTLEMENT OF PORTUS.

Forum Baths

Arcades near the Forum Baths

UNDER THE EMPEROR DOMITIAN (81-96), LIFE AT OSTIA HAD A NEW IMPULSE: THE TOWN WAS FOR THE MOST PART RESTORED WITH A 1 METRE RAISING OF THE ROAD SURFACE, PERHAPS ALSO FOR THE BUILDING OF HIGHER PALACES, WHICH NEEDED DEEPER FOUNDATIONS, AS THEY WERE BUILT ON SANDY AND FILLING EARTH. THE TERME DI NETTUNO, THE CASERMA DEI VIGILI, (REBUILT LATER ON), THE CURIA AND THE BASILICA DATE TO THIS PERIOD BUT WERE COMPLETED BY TRAJAN (98-117). THIS LAST EMPEROR RESTORED ALSO THE AREAS ON THE WEST SIDE OF THE TOWN, IN THE AREA AT THE FORK OF THE DECUMANUS AND VIA DELLA FOCE.

BUT THE MOST IMPORTANT TRAJANIAN WORK ON THE SEASHORE WAS THE ENLARGEMENT OF THE TOWN OF PORTUS WITH THE BUILDING OF AN HEXAGONAL BASIN, UNIQUE IN THE HARBOUR HISTORY OF THE MEDITERRANEAN. IT WAS JOINED TO THE TIBER AND TO THE SEA BY A CANAL DUG BY HIS PREDECESSOR CLAUDIUS AND RESTORED BY HIMSELF. PORTO BECAME THE MOST IMPORTANT TOWN OF THE COAST, FROM A COMMERCIAL POINT OF VIEW, WHILE OSTIA HOUSED OFFICES, ADMINISTRATIVE BUILDINGS AND CULT EDIFICES.

UNDER HADRIAN (117-138) - WHO ALSO BUILT THE PANTHEON IN ROME AND HIS MAGNIFICENT VILLA AT TIVOLI - AND HIS SUCCESSOR ANTONINUS PIUS (138-161), THE APEX OF PROSPERITY WAS REACHED. THE AREA TO THE NORTH OF THE FORUM AND THAT AROUND THE CASERMA DEI VIGILI WAS BUILT; THE HOUSES WITH GARDENS NEAR PORTA MARINA WERE REALISED; THE DWELLING HOUSES - AMONG WHICH THOSE OF THE SERAPIS, THE CASA DI DIANA AND OF THE AURIGHI - DEVELOPED HERE; ALSO NEW HORREA (DEPOSITS, WAREHOUSES) WERE CREATED - AMONG THEM THOSE OF THE HEPAGATHIANA. OSTIA REACHED SOME 50,000 INHABITANTS, WHILE ROME HAD A POPULATION OF A MILLION INHABITANTS.

ALSO UNDER MARCUS AURELIUS (161-180) AND COMMODUS (180-192), THE AREA WAS CHARACTERISED BY SO MUCH GREAT SPLENDOUR THAT IT WAS CALLED "COLONIA FELIX COMMODIANA".

FROM SEPTIMIUS SEVERUS (193-211) TO CARACALLA (211-217) ONLY RESTORATIONS WERE CARRIED ON, BUT IT WAS IN THIS PERIOD THAT VIA SEVERIANA WAS BUILT, TO LINK OSTIA TO PORTO AND TERRACINA.

THE TEMPIO ROTONDO WAS STARTED UNDER ALEXANDER SEVERUS (222-235) AND WAS COMPLETED IN THE MIDDLE OF THE CENTURY - IT IS THE SO-CALLED "SWAN SONG" OF OSTIA MONUMENTAL BUILDING ACTIVITIES.

THE DECLINE

OSTIA BEGAN TO DECLINE SLOWLY, LIKE THE WHOLE WESTERN ROMAN EMPIRE, SINCE THE SECOND HALF OF THE III CENTURY (ROME WAS FORTIFIED AGAINST PROBABLE ATTACKS FROM THE BARBARIANS, IN 272 AD). UNDER DIOCLETIAN (284-305) AND CONSTAN-

TINE (312-337) THERE WERE SOME PERIODS OF REVIVAL - THEY RESTORED SOME PUBLIC BUILD-
INGS, SUCH AS BATHS AND TEMPLES, EVEN THOUGH THEY FAVOURED THE DEVELOPMENT OF
THE TOWN OF PORTO, WHICH WAS THEN CALLED CIVITAS FLAVIA CONSTANTINIANA POR-
TUENSIS.

IN 330, THE IMPERIAL SEAT WAS MOVED FROM ROME TO CONSTANTINOPLE AND THEN IN 402
RAVENNA BECAME THE CAPITAL OF THE WESTERN ROMAN EMPIRE. OSTIA BEGAN A FASTER
DECLINE.

AT THE END OF THE 4TH CENTURY SOME MAGNIFICENT DOMUS WERE BUILT IN RESTORED
HOUSES DATING FROM THE I AND II C. THEN IN 410 THE TOWN WAS SACKED BY THE VISI-
GOTHS AND IN 455 BY THE VANDALS OF GENSERIC.

IN 537 THE SEASHORES WERE OCCUPIED BY THE GOTHS DURING THE WARS LED BY JUSTINIA-
NUS TO RECONQUER ITALY. THIS IS THE DESCRIPTION OF THE PLACE BY PROCOPIO DI CESA-
REA IN HIS "GOTHIC WAR" (MID 6TH C): "TO THE LEFT, BEFORE THE OTHER MOUTH OF THE
TIBER, LIES OSTIA, A TOWN NOT ONLY WORTHY OF THE RIVER SHORE, BUT ALSO OF THE
HIGHEST PRAISE. NOW IT IS UNPROVIDED OF WALLS", AND THE VIA OSTIENSE IS NOW
"WOODY AND NEGLECTED" (BOOK I, CHAP.XXVI).

FURTHER NEWS ABOUT THIS PART OF THE SEASHORE CAN BE FOUND IN THE WORK BY POPE
GREGORY IV (824-844) WHO, TO PROTECT IT FROM SARACEN RAIDS, FOUNDED A FORTIFIED
AREA, NAMED AFTER HIMSELF - GREGORIOPOLI. IT MAY NOW BE IDENTIFIED WITH THE PRE-
SENT VILLAGE BEYOND VIA OSTIENSE, WHERE THE CHURCH OF ST.AUREA AND THE RENAISS-
ANCE FORTRESS STAND.

AS ROME WAS DESPOILED OF ITS ANCIENT MONUMENTS, SO WE KNOW THAT IN THE 11TH
CENTURY OSTIA MARBLES WERE USED TO BUILD THE DUOMO OF ORVIETO AND THE MAGNIFI-
CENT BUILDINGS IN PIAZZA DEI MIRA-
COLI IN PISA: IT EVIDENCES HOW THE
ANCIENT TOWN WAS NEGLECTED.

IN 1461 POPE PIUS II PICCOLOMINI
VISITED THE TOWN AND WROTE IN HIS
COMMENTARII:" ONCE IT WAS SURELY
A GREAT TOWN -JUST LOOK AT THE
RUINS EXTENDING IN A VERY LARGE
AREA. (...)YOU CAN STILL SEE PORTI-
COES IN RUIN, LAYING COLUMNS AND
FRAGMENTS OF STATUES" (BOOK XI,
48-51). THE ANCIENT TOWN OF
OSTIA REMAINED IN THIS STATE OF
NEGLECT AND DECAY TILL THE END
OF THE 19TH CENTURY. SINCE 1884
ALL THE SEASHORES WERE RECLAIMED
AND, SINCE THE FIRST YEARS OF THE
1900S, THE NEW CORE OF OSTIA
MARITTIMA WAS FOUNDED 2 KM FAR
(THE PRESENT LIDO DI OSTIA IS AN
AREA ADMINISTRATIVELY DEPENDING
FROM THE COMUNE DI ROMA).

Late-ancient composite capital

THE EXCAVATIONS

THE VERY FIRST AND SPORADIC EXCAVATIONS OF OSTIA OCCURRED AT THE END OF THE 1700S. THEN, POPE PIUS VII (1800-23) STARTED A SYSTEMATICAL CAMPAIGN IN 1805, FOLLOWED BY POPE PIUS IX (1846-78) SINCE 1870, THAT IS TEN YEARS AFTER THE UNITY OF ITALY. THESE TASKS WERE LED BY THE EMINENT ROMAN ARCHAEOLOGIST RODOLFO LANCIANI.

OTHER CAMPAIGNS WERE CARRIED ON IN 1909 AND FROM 1938 TO 1942 (ON THE OCCASION OF THE UNIVERSAL EXHIBITION WHICH HAD TO BE HELD IN ROME IN THAT SAME YEAR, BUT IT WAS CANCELLED BECAUSE OF THE WAR); IN THIS LAST PHASE TWO THIRDS OF THE TOWN OF OSTIA WERE BROUGHT TO LIGHT, UNDER THE GUIDE OF THE ARCHAEOLOGIST GUIDO CALZA. IN THOSE YEARS, IN COMPLIANCE WITH FASCIST PROPAGANDA, ALMOST ALL THE RUINS VISIBLE TODAY WERE UNCOVERED FEVERISHLY. AS HAS HAPPENED IN ROME IN THE EXCAVATIONS OF

View of the ruins

THE IMPERIAL FORUM, STACKS OF EARTH AND DETRITUS WERE QUICKLY REMOVED. THEY WOULD HAVE PROVED THE LATE ANCIENT DECAY OF OSTIA, IF THEY HAD BEEN APPROPRIATELY STUDIED. THE RESTORATIONS TENDING TO MAKE THE RUINS MORE "COMPLETE" AND "TRUE" WERE VERY DEEP AND SOMETIMES SPOILED THE ANCIENT STRUCTURES. TO UNDERSTAND HOW SOME WORKS WERE CARRIED ON, IT IS INTERESTING TO REREAD A REPORT OF 1941 BY THE SAME ARCHAEOLOGIST: "PROCEEDING IN THE DISCOVERY OF THE MONUMENTS AND BUILDINGS, THEY ARE CONSOLIDATED IN THEIR DECAYING STRUCTURE AND BROUGHT TO THEIR PRIMITIVE STATUS, THROUGH THE RESTORATION OF THE FALLEN PIECES, THE STANDING OF THE COLUMNS AND THE CLEANING OF THE MOSAICS AND PAINTINGS, WHICH HAVE TO BE REMOVED FROM THE FLOORS AND WALLS TO ACQUIRE THEIR PRIMITIVE STRENGTH (...).

TODAY THE METHOD USED IN THE EXCAVATION IS VERY DIFFERENT: YOU START FROM THE FACT THAT EACH "LAYER" IS A WITNESS OF A PHASE OF OUR HISTORY AND, BEFORE BEING ERASED FOR EVER, IT MUST BE STUDIED, DRAWN AND PHOTOGRAPHED. THIS TECHNIQUE IS CALLED "STRATIGRAPHIC LAYER" AND THIS LETS YOU ASSEMBLE THE MOST DOCUMENTS TO PROCEED INTO A DEEP KNOWLEDGE OF THE PAST.

FEATURES OF THE ROMAN TOWN PLANNING

EXCAVATIONS HAVE HELPED TO DEFINE AN URBANISTIC STRUCTURE TYPICAL OF ALL ROMAN TOWNS. THEY WERE BORN LIKE "CASTRUM", THAT IS FORTIFIED PLACES: THEY WERE CROSSED BY A CARDO (NORTH-SOUTH AXIS) AND A DECUMANUS (WEST-EAST AXIS), AT WHOSE JUNCTION THERE WAS A SQUARE CALLED FORUM (FROM LATIN "FORAS", THAT IS "OUTSIDE", BECAUSE THE FIRST PUBLIC AREA OF ROME, THE "FORUM BOARIUM", WAS SITUATED OUTSIDE

THE INHABITED CENTRE). THE MAIN BUILD-
INGS, SUCH AS TEMPLES, BASILICAS AND
GENERAL PUBLIC EDIFICES WERE ERECTED
HERE. THE OTHER ROADS OF THE ROMAN
TOWN WERE PERPENDICULAR OR PARALLEL TO
THE CARDO AND THE DECUMANUS, THUS FORM-
ING SQUARE AND REGULAR HOUSES. SOMETI-
MES, THIS TYPICAL "RETICULUS" WAS INTER-
RUPTED BY THE OBLIQUE LINES OF PRE-EXIST-
ING PATHS, WHICH WANTED TO BE REMEMBERED.
AT THE TWO MAIN AXES, THE WALLS HAD
MONUMENTAL ENTRANCES. OSTIA WAS LIKE
THIS. IN THE TOWN PLANNING YOU MAY SEE
TWO STRUCTURES, ONE INSIDE THE OTHER:
THE FIRST - 4TH CENTURY BC -PRESENTED
WALLS MADE OF LAYERS OF BIG STONE BLOCKS
("OPUS QUADRATUM"); THE SECOND WAS LATER

Decumanus

AND CONCENTRIC TO THE FIRST, SURROUNDED BY BRICK WALLS DATING FROM THE 80 BC WITH
THREE STILL EXISTING OPEN GATES IN VIA OSTIENSE (PORTA ROMANA), IN VIA LAURENTINA
(PORTA LAURENTINA) AND THE DECUMANUS MAXIMUS (PORTA MARINA); TOWARDS THE RIVER
THERE WERE NO FORTIFIED STRUCTURES. OF COURSE THE NAMES OF THE ENTRANCE GATES ARE
MODERN.
SINCE THE II CENTURY BC, THE TOWN DEVELOPED IN THIS AREA AND IN ITS MOST IMPORTANT
MOMENT (II-III CENTURY AD) IT HAD, AS ALREADY SAID, SOME 50,000 INHABITANTS,
WAREHOUSES, MARKETS, BIG DWELLING HOUSES, TEMPLES, BASILICAS, NYMPHAEUMS AND BATHS.

FEATURES OF ROMAN ARCHITECTURE

T HE BUILDINGS USUALLY HAD A SQUARE OR RECTANGULAR REGULAR PLAN, WITH PARALLEL
    WALLS AND CONSTANT THICKNESS. THEIR HEIGHT WAS VARIABLE: ALTHOUGH THE SANDY
GROUND OF OSTIA, THE DWELLING HOUSES (INSULAE) WERE EVEN FIVE-STOREY HIGH. THE
ROAD LINES WERE ALWAYS RESPECTED AND ON THE PRINCIPAL ARTERIES THERE WERE WIDE
ARCADES WITH TABERNAE (SHOPS).
SYMMETRY AND REGULARITY WERE SOMETIMES INTERRUPTED BY PARTICULAR BUILDINGS, SUCH
AS TEMPLES (RECTANGULAR OR MORE SELDOM WITH A CENTRAL OPEN SPACE), BATHS (WITH
MIXTILINEAR OR OVAL CIRCULAR ROOMS), OR THEATRES WITH THEIR CLASSICAL SEMICIRCULAR
SHAPE.
THE ROMANS WERE VERY SKILLED BUILDERS AND LARGELY USED THE VAULTS: THE BARREL ONE
PARTICULARLY SUITABLE FOR RECTANGULAR AREAS, OR THE CROSS VAULT FOR SQUARE SPACES.
AT OSTIA THERE IS A ROUND BUILDING OF THE FIRST HALF OF THE III CENTURY, WHICH IS SUPPOSED
TO BE COVERED WITH A DOME SIMILAR TO THAT OF THE PANTHEON IN ROME. VAULTS AND
DOMES WERE DONE IN OPUS CAEMENTITIUM (SEE THE "BUILDING TECHNIQUES" SECTION).
AMPHORAS STUCK ONE ON TOP OF THE OTHER AND DIPPED INTO THE CONGLOMERATE WERE
USED TO LIGHTER THEM, ABOVE ALL IN THE LATE AGE (III-IV CENTURY).

RELIGIOUS CULTS AT OSTIA

Sacello of the Lares Augusti

At Ostia, as it was in Rome, there were numerous cult buildings dedicated to very different divinities. The most ancient sanctuaries date back to the Republican age (IV - I century BC) and were ranged around two main places: the first, near the theatre, was made of four small temples on one podium, probably dedicated to Venus (goddess of love and beauty), Fortuna, Ceres (goddess of harvest and nature) and to Hope; the second place was near the junction of the Decumanus and Via della Foce and included a temple dedicated to Hercules (god of strength and courage), and two other small temples dedicated to Aesculapius (god of medicine) and Igea (goddess of health). In the forum there was the Capitolium, which is the biggest temple, dedicated to the Roman triad which include Jupiter (father of gods and men), Mars (god of war) and Juno (mother and queen of the Heaven, Jupiter's sister and wife, protectress of women and families). The front building was dedicated to the Goddess Roma, while a circular temple was probably devoted to the cult of all gods, like the Roman Pantheon.

At Ostia the cult of Vulcan (god of fire and protector from fires) was in higher favour; his most important priest - the Pontifex Vulcani - was the religious leader of the town. The temple dedicated to him has not been found.

Literary sources let us know that also the Gemini were object of cult: Castor and Pollux were Zeus' sons and protectors of navigation. Their temple has never been found. Some emperors were also adored like Gods: Augustus and Trajan, whose priests were gathered in "collegia". In the Roman world also the cults imported from eastern countries were numerous: many devotees were to be found amongst traders, soldiers and slaves brought to Rome from conquered countries. The most important cult was Mithraism, deriving from Indian and Persian regions. It spread in Italy since the I century AD and had a great impulse at the end of the II and in the III century; in the IV century it disappeared because the Christian

RELIGION BECAME STATE RELIGION. MITHRAISM WAS PRACTISED ONLY BY MEN AND IT ATTRIBUTED TO GOD MITHRAS - IDENTIFIED WITH THE SUN - THE CREATION OF COSMOS: THROUGH THE SACRIFICE OF A BULL, HE WOULD HAVE GIVEN BIRTH TO ANIMALS AND PLANTS, WHILE THE SOUL OF THE MORTAL BEINGS IS SUPPOSED TO HAVE BEEN INCARNATED IN MEN AFTER HAVING CROSSED THE SPHERES OF THE SEVEN PLANETS; INITIATION CONSISTED IN SEVEN STEPS OF ASCENT AND REQUIRED A CORRECT MORAL BEHAVIOUR. THERE ARE STRIKING COINCIDENCES WITH CHRISTIANITY: MITHRAS WAS BORN IN A CAVE ON THE 25TH DECEMBER AND WAS VENERATED ON SUNDAYS. IMPORTANT RITES WERE BAPTISM, CONFIRMATION AND EXTREME UNCTION.

18 MITHRAEUMS HAVE BEEN FOUND IN THE PART DUG UNTIL NOW AT OSTIA; ALL OF THEM WERE SITUATED IN THE DARKEST CORNERS OF PRE-EXISTING BUILDINGS USED AS HORREA, BATHS OR INSULAE - JUST TO REMIND THE ORIGINAL CAVE. THEY DATE FROM THE II AND THE III CENTURY. USUALLY THEY WERE NARROW AND LONG PLACES, WITH SIDE PODIUMS WHERE THE DEVOTEES LAID DOWN; IN THE CENTRAL CORRIDOR PASSED THE PROCESSION TO THE ALTAR, WHERE MITHRA TAUROCTONO WAS REPRESENTED, SIDED BY THE TWO GENES CAUTES AND CAUTOPATES, SYMBOLS OF DAY AND NIGHT. ACCORDING TO SOME HISTORIANS, THERE WERE SOME 40 MITHRAEUMS AT OSTIA, AS MITHRAISM WAS THE SECOND MOST PRACTISED CULT, AFTER PAGANISM.

OTHER ORIENTAL DIVINITIES WERE ADORED IN THE ROMAN WORLD AND THEN ALSO AT OSTIA, SUCH AS:

1. SABATIUS, DIVINITY FROM FRIGIA, A REGION IN ASIA MINOR, CONQUERED IN THE 6TH CENTURY BY THE PERSIANS AND PASSED UNDER THE ROMAN DOMINION, SINCE THE II CENTURY. THIS GODDESS WAS ADORED ALSO IN ANCIENT GREECE WITH ORGIASTIC RITES. IN THE ROMAN WORLD HER CULT FUSED WITH THAT OF MOTHERS. THE SANCTUARY, SITUATED ON THE DECUMANUS, NEAR THE CASERMA DEI VIGILI, WAS IN THE CITY CENTRE AND, LIKE THE MITHRAEUMS, IN A CORNER OF A BUILDING.

2. SERAPIS, EGYPTIAN GODDESS ARTIFICIALLY CREATED BY KING TOLOMEUS I OF EGYPT (304-283) TO GIVE A PROTECTRESS GODDESS TO THE TOWN OF ALEXANDRIA. THE OSTIA SANCTUARY, CALLED SERAPÉO, WAS SITUATED ON THE WESTERN OUTSKIRTS OF THE TOWN, BETWEEN THE SEA AND THE RIVER.

3. BELLONA, ANCIENT LATIN GODDESS OF WAR. NEAR HER SANCTUARIES WARS WERE DECLARED (PROBABLY THERE IS AN ANALOGY WITH THE LATIN ETYMON BELLUM = WAR); DURING THE II AND III CENTURY IT WAS FUSED WITH MA, A GODDESS FROM ASIA MINOR, WHOSE DEVOTEES PRACTISED RITES

Mithraeum of the Baths

Small pagan temple

INFLICTING INJURIES UPON THEMSELVES.

4. ATTIS, SHEPHERD GOD FROM FRIGIA, TOO. ACCORDING TO TRADITION HE FELL IN LOVE WITH CYBELE, PROTECTRESS OF FERTILITY ON EARTH, KNOWN ALSO AS MAGNA MATER AND EMASCULATED FOR LOVE: AFTER THAT, HE RAISED FROM DEATH AS A PINE TREE; HENCE THE CUSTOM OF HIS PRIESTS TO MUTILATE THEMSELVES. BAPTISM WAS MADE WITH THE SACRIFICE OF A BULL, LIKE IN MITHRAISM: THE NEW FOLLOWER WAS LAID IN A HOLE AND OVER HIM, ON SCAFFOLDINGS, A SLAUGHTERED BULL SPRINKLED HIM WITH BLOOD, PURIFYING HIM. HIS FEAST DAY WAS CELEBRATED FROM MARCH 15TH TO THE 17TH AND THE II CENTURY AD SANCTUARY IN THE TYPICAL TRIANGLE SQUARE WAS SITUATED NEAR THE PORTA LAURENTINA, ISOLATED FROM THE REST OF THE TOWN AND IT CONTAINED THE SANCTUARY OF ATTIS AND THE TEMPLE OF CYBELE.

5. ISIS, DIVINITY FROM EGYPT, WAS THE PROTECTRESS OF SAILORS, THE GODDESS OF FERTILITY AND QUEEN OF AFTERLIFE. SHE WAS OSIRIDE'S SISTER AND WIFE AND WAS REPRESENTED WITH

A CROWN MADE OF BOVINE HORNS SURROUNDING A DISK. WORTH REMEMBERING IS THAT, UNDER EMPEROR CALIGULA (37-41), A GREAT TEMPLE WAS ERECTED IN HER HONOR IN ROME, NEAR THE PANTHEON. NO TRACES HAVE BEEN FOUND OF BUILDINGS USED FOR THIS CULT AT OSTIA OR IN PORTO, EVEN IF WE ARE SURE OF THEIR EXISTENCES. HER FEAST DAY WAS CELEBRATED ON MARCH 5TH, AT THE BEGINNING OF SPRING.

AT OSTIA THERE WAS ALSO A STRONG HEBRAIC COMMUNITY, WHO BUILT, IN THE MIDDLE OF THE I CENTURY AD, AN IMPORTANT SYNAGOGUE, WHICH WILL BE RESTORED IN THE 4TH CENTURY, IN THE SAME PERIOD IN WHICH THE DECAY OF THE TOWN BEGINS. THE PRESENCE OF JEWS IN ROME DATES BACK TO THE III-II CENTURY BC, ALTHOUGH THERE ARE NO FINDS, WHEN THERE WAS A GREAT MIGRAT-

Synagogue

ION FROM PALESTINE TO EGYPT, SYRIA, ASIA MINOR, GREECE AND ALSO ITALY. THEY WERE MERCHANTS SEEKING THEIR FORTUNE OUTSIDE THEIR LAND, GIVING BIRTH, SOMETIMES, TO RELEVANT COMMUNITIES, SUCH AS THAT OF ALEXANDRIA OF EGYPT. OTHER JEWS ARRIVED FORCEDLY IN ROME IN 63 BC, WHEN THE ROMAN TROOPS OF POMPEY ENTERED JERUSALEM, AND DEPORTED NUMEROUS SLAVES TO ROME. SOME OF THEM WERE SOON

Christian Basilica

REDEEMED BY OTHER JEWS, ALSO BECAUSE THEY WERE DISLIKED BY THEIR OWNERS, AS THEY DID NOT WANT TO WORK ON SATURDAYS AND ASKED FOR PARTICULAR FOOD. SO THEY BECAME "LIBERTI", THAT IS FREED SLAVES. UNDER VESPASIAN (69-79) AND TITUS (79-81) THERE WERE OTHER SAD ENLARGEMENTS IN THE JEWISH COMMUNITY, AS THEY CONQUERED PALESTINE. AT THE BEGINNING OF THE I CENTURY AD, ROME IS SUPPOSED TO HOST 30,000-40,000 JEWS AND A POPULATION OF 1,000,000 INHABITANTS; OSTIA HAD A COMMUNITY OF 2,000-3,000 PEOPLE, ALL OF THEM TRADERS AND MERCHANTS. SINCE THE SECOND HALF OF THE 4TH CENTURY THE CHRISTIAN CULT ESTABLISHED SLOWLY IN OSTIA AND PORTO. IT IS SAID THAT THIS LATE PRESENCE IS DUE TO THE PERSISTENCE OF MITHRAISM AND THE NUMEROUS ORIENTAL RELIGIONS WHICH STILL EXISTED. INSIDE THE EXCAVATIONS THERE ARE THREE PRESENCES OF THE CHRISTIAN CULT:

- A BASILICA WITH TWO AISLES ON THE DECUMANUS, BEYOND THE JUNCTION OF VIA DELLA FOCE;
- A MITHRAEUM WITH CHRISTIAN INSCRIPTIONS;
- TRACES OF A VERY ANCIENT BASILICA, ST. CYRIACUS, BUILT OVER A NYMPHAEUM, NEAR THE THEATRE.

WE KNOW THAT ST. AUGUSTINE (354-430) STOPPED AT OSTIA WHILE ABOUT TO EMBARK FOR TUNISIA, HIS BELOVED LAND. HE WAS WITH HIS MOTHER MONICA, WHO, ALREADY ILL, DIED AND WAS BURIED IN THE SAME PLACE WHERE THE CHURCH OF S. AUREA WAS ERECTED AT THE END OF THE 15TH CENTURY.

Traces of the Christian Basilica of St. Cyriacus

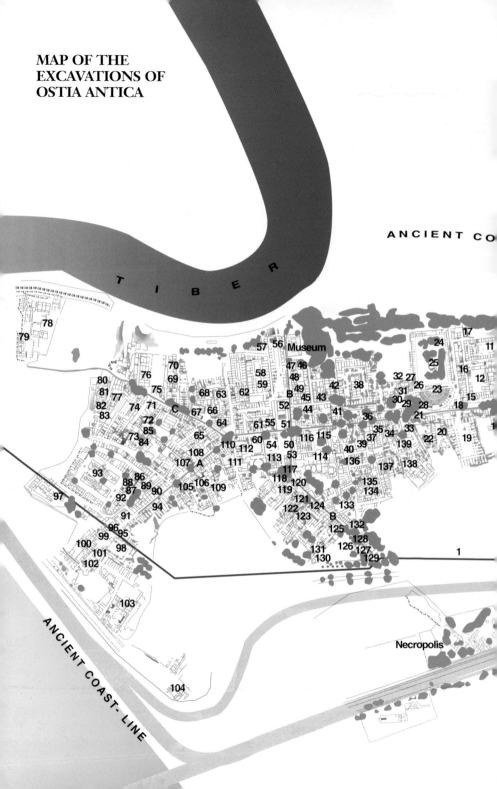

N

OF THE TIBER

77) Terme della Trinacria
78) Imperial Palace
79) Mithraeum
80) Caseggiato di Bacco e Arianna
81) Tempio di Serapide
82) Mithraeum della Planta Pedis
83) Warehouse of the Dolia
84) Sacello of the three aisles
85) Calcara
86) Insula delle Muse
87) Insula del Graffito
88) Insula delle Pareti Gialle
89) Insula delle volte dipinte
90) Insula delle Trifore
91) Domus del Ninfeo
92) Domus dei Dioscuri
93) Case Giardino
94) Caseggiato della Fontana con Lucerna
95) Caupona di Alexander
96) Porta Marina
97) Maritime Baths
98) Forum di Porta Marina
99) Burial Monument
100) Domus Fulminata
101) Sanctuary della Bona Dea
102) Sepulchre of Cartilius Poplicola
103) Baths of Porta Marina
104) Synagogue
105) Caseggiato delle Tabernae Finestrate
106) Schola of Trajan
107) Tempio dei Fabbri Navali
108) Christian Basilica
109) Mithraeum delle Sette Porte
110) Taberna dei Pescivendoli
111) Tempio di Iside
112) Collegial Temple
113) Domus del Tempio Rotondo
114) Forum Baths
115) Forum della Statua Eroica
116) Caseggiato dei Triclini
117) Forica
118) Domus di Giove Fulminatore
119) House with a mosaic niche
120) Nymphaeum degli Eroti
121) Domus delle Colonne
122) Domus dei Pesci
123) Caupona del Pavona
124) Caseggiato di Ercole
125) Terme del Faro
126) Campo della Magna Mater
127) Sanctuary of Attis
128) Schola degli Hastiferi
129) Tempio di Bellona
130) Tempio di Cybele
131) Mithraeum degli Animali
132) Domus di Medusa
133) Molino
134) Domus del Protiro
135) Terme del Filosofo
136) Domus della Fortuna Annonaria
137) Caseggiato dei Lottatori
138) Mithraeum del Felicissimo
139) Fullonica
140) Necropolis
141) Renaissance Borgo
A) Decumanus
B) Cardo
C) Via della Foce

1) Sullan Walls
2) Porta Romana
3) Piazzale della Vittoria
4) Caseggiato del cane Monnus
5) Republican warehouses
6) Terme dei Cisarii
7) Mithraeum
8) Arcades
9) Warehouses
10) Mosaic in Via dei Vigili
11) Caserma dei Vigili
12) Terme di Nettuno
13) Arcades with shops
14) Sabazéo
15) Caupona del Fortunato
16) Insula del Soffitto Dipinto
17) Fullonica
18) Christian Oratory
19) Horrea di Ortensio
20) Horrea dell'Artemide
21) Republican Monument
22) Ration or Dolia Warehouse
23) Theatre
24) Forum delle Corporazioni
25) Tempio di Cerere
26) Ara dei Gemelli
27) Domus di Apuleio
28) Semicircular Nymphaeum
29) Sacello di Giove
30) Nymphaeum with three apses
31) Small Republican temples
32) Mithraeum delle Sette Sfere
33) Collegial Temple
34) Seat of the Augustali
35) Mithraeum dei Serpenti
36) Hall of Mars and Venus
37) Caseggiato del Sole
38) Big Horrea
39) Terme dell'Invidioso
40) Insula dell'Invidioso
41) Ancient Castrum walls
42) Bakery
43) Caseggiato di Diana
44) Thermopolium
45) Insula di Giove e Ganimede
46) Mithraeum di Lucrezio Menandro
47) Caseggiato dei Doli
48) Insula dei Dipinti
49) Insula di Bacco fanciullo
50) Forum
51) Republican Temple
52) Capitolium
53) Tempio di Roma e Augusto
54) Basilica
55) Curia
56) Caseggiato con Balconi a mensole
57) Caseggiato dei Misuratori di grano
58) Portico of the small market
59) Small market
60) Tempio Rotondo
61) Caseggiato del Larario
62) Horrea Epagathiana
63) Terme del Buticoso
64) Caseggiato del Mosaico di Porto
65) Mithraeum delle Pareti Dipinte
66) Area of the Republican Temples
67) Tempio dell'Ara Rotonda
68) Domus di Amore e Psiche
69) Baths
70) Mithraeum of the Baths
71) Caseggiato del Serapide
72) Terme dei Sette Sapienti
73) Caseggiato degli Aurighi
74) Casette Tipo
75) Aula dei Mensores
76) Horrea

Marble block with greetings
to a Roman emperor

A s soon as you enter, you will be in the final part of
Via Ostiense (the artery linking to Rome), sided by
the Necropolis (see pages 64/65). You are not yet in town,
which started farther on, from Porta Romana. Before the
ruins of the Porta, on the right, you can read an inscription
on a marble block which once was the base of a statue:
SALUTI CAESARIS AUGUST(I) GLABRIO PATRO-
NUS COLONIAE D(onum) D(edit) F(amili) (a)C(ilii) (=
to the safety of Caesar Augustus, Glabrio patron of the
colony). It refers to a certain Glabrio of the Acilii family
who saluted an emperor of the I century AD, visiting Ostia.
Then you see the remains of the town walls, dating to the
first period of their construction in the I century BC (they
are big tufa blocks situated slightly below the road level);
emperor Domitian (81-96) will rebuild them, when all the
road surface was raised of about 1 metre. These fortified
walls, dug for 1.8 km, enclosed a great part of Ostia houses
and presented three gates: Porta Romana, named after its
location on Via Ostiense, leading to Rome; Porta Laurentina, on the road directed southwards, where was situated the
town of Laurentum and Porta Marina towards the sea.
There were not fortified walls along the banks of the river.
The one-arched Porta Romana was sided by two square
towers with very few remains. On the external pediment
there was probably a great marble slab (now located soon
beyond the gate to the left) with an inscription about the build-

Slab with a dedicated inscription

ing of the walls by the Senate and the people of the Ostia colony:"SENATUS POPULUSQUE COLONIAE OSTIENSIUM MUROS DEDIT".

You are then in Piazzale della Vittoria, where most likely men and horse chariots coming from Rome stopped to have some refreshments. Here there was a nymphaeum of the 4th century AD and a statue of

Piazzale della Vittoria

winged Victory representing Minerva, goddess of town freedom: it dates from the end of the I century AD and may once have adorned the town gate together with a similar one. To the right is a polychrome mosaic with a geometric pattern, dating from the end of the III c. and probably belonging to a house discovered in the middle of the 19th c., but now disappeared.

The first buildings to the right of the Decumanus, one of the two main axes in town, are:

- the Caseggiato del cane Monnus, named after a mosaic with a dog and the inscription Monnus. The building dates from the beginning of the II c., the mosaic from the III c.
- the so-called "Republican " warehouses used for the storage of goods- note the walls in opus quadratum. They were rebuilt in the I c. AD, under the reign of Hadrian (117-138), the northern part was transformed into a thermal building called Terme dei Cisarii (from Latin "cisium" = chariot) for the presence of many chariot scenes; the structure was surely reserved to those workers. It is interesting to notice the mosaic of the "frigidarium" or cold water pool, representing the square walls with towers and four male statues on the sides; below there are horse chariots and marine mythological figures. Worth a note is the restoration, consisting in the completing of the walls and the semicylinder coverings with a horizontal line at the base, engraved in the mortar, to separate the ancient from the new. In the south-eastern corner of the building there was a Mithraeum, dedicated to the cult of God Mithras. It dates from the III c. AD but it is very badly preserved, as only the two lateral podiums and the foundations of the altar stand still (see the insert on the cults).

Victory statue

Mosaic in the Terme dei Cisarii

the Decumanus, the Caserma dei Vigili and the Terme di Nettuno

The Decumanus

Well on the Decumanus

Then go back along the Decumanus, once surrounded by porticoes on both sides: they were a covered passage lined with shops. To the right, behind the remains of the arcades of which only the inferior parts of the pillars still stand (first half of the II c. AD), there were warehouses and intensive houses. The area to the left will be soon object of excavation.

Along the road, some gratings let us see the lead pipes conveying water to the town; near the Caserma dei Vigili in the centre of the road there is a well of the V c. which points out that the Decumanus and the town were abandoned in a late age, as witnessed by the presence of a structure in the centre of the road to draw water from. (Rome had been invaded by the Visigoths led by Alaric in 410 and in 455 by the Vandals who had attacked the mouths of the Tiber from the sea).

Turning left to Via dei Vigili and leaving the Terme where you will soon return, we suggest that you go to the Caserma which gives its name to the road.

To the left you will note a cistern and, a bit farther on, to the right, a nice mosaic of the 40-50 AD, deriving from baths built before those of Neptune (II century). Worth noting is how the excavation has stressed the works of different periods to prove the stratifications during the time. In the central rectangle there are 4 dolphins sided by 8 symbolic figures. From the left: a winged head (symbol of the wind), a female face with trunk (= symbol of Africa) and a male one with a crocodile (=Egypt), then one more male profile with wings (=another wind). On the right there is: a square with three legs (symbol of Sicily, because this land is characterised by three promontories), other two with winged heads (other winds) and an olive crowned head (symbol of Spain, where oil was imported from). Archaeologists have

Mosaic in Via dei Vigili

connected those subjects to the building of the port of Claudius, farther north, where ships sailed towards those directions. All around, there are squares representing various shields alternated with geometric patterns.

The Caserma dei Vigili, perhaps built for the first time under emperor Domitian (81-96), was renovated in 130 under Hadrian and then restored again at the beginning of the III century by Septimius Severus and Caracalla. On the main prospect, before entering the building, you will find: to the left corner space, a latrine (1), and in the three rooms on the sides of the entrance, two on the left and one on the right, rooms for the pouring out of wine (2). On that on the left you can read the name Paulus. A vestibule leads you to what remains of an arcade (3) and then to the wide central rectangular courtyard measuring m.41 x 70; in the corners towards the entrance there are two fountains (4), while in the back you may see the remains of an altar, called Caesa-

reum, where imperial divinities were adored (5). The mosaic represents the sacrifice of a bull in three different phases: in the centre, near the altar, unfortunately incomplete, is represented a bull bound and raging; on the right his exhaustion and on the left his decisive killing. In the origin the Caserma was two-storey high and presents interesting rests of the stairs leading upwards. The building had a very regular and rational arrangement of the rooms; behind the altar there were five areas alike: most likely they were lodgings reserved to the officials. To the back there was a latrine and some regular shops lined on Via della Fontana. Return then to the Decumanus to visit the Terme di Nettuno, the entrance of some rooms of which was on Via dei Vigili. They were built by Hadrian (117-138) on pre-existing baths built by Domitian (81-96), and then restored at the end of the II and IV century AD. Around a wide rectangular arcade court on three sides there are various areas: the atrium with the magnificent mosaic giving its name to the complex (1), (still visible from the platform entered through by the Decumanus); then the pools in the typical Roman position: the frigidarium (2) with cold water, the tepidarium (3) with warm water and the calidarium (4) with hot water; to the other side, to the left of the arcade courtyard, there are additional spaces.

Entering from Via dei Vigili, through a small gate you will see, to the left, the wide area of the frigidarium with two granite columns with Corinthian capitals: the pools were on the sides, while

The Vigili (Wardens) Corps

The Corps of the Vigili already existed in the Republican period and worked as nightly road wardens and with slaves who had to put out fires. The group was reorganised by Augustus (23 BC - 14 AD) with the introduction of public servants in 22 BC and then in 6 AD with real patrols. The leader was a praefectus vigilum who had to co-ordinate all the activities, to judge fire crimes, thefts, damages, excluding the serious offences which were judged by the praefectus urbis with the capital punishment. In Rome there were 7,000 vigili, in 7 barracks and guard places - not all the buildings have been located. At Ostia there were 700 men, depending from the central office of Rome.

To understand the real importance of this corps just think that most of the town was made of wood, that the buildings were very close and that fire was used to cook, heat and light. Fires in town were very usual. The protector of the Vigili was Vulcan, the god of fire, and Stata Mater, a goddess who protected from fires.

TERME DI NETTUNO

Terme di Nettuno

in the centre is preserved a wide mosaic representing the Nereids (=nymphs of the sea), Tritons (sea-gods with human body and fish tail), sea snakes and hippocampi (small sea horses). Then you pass two heated areas, where the warm pools were. On the walls you may still see the holed terracotta pipes conveying hot air to the rooms: they came from underground rooms, where slaves worked to bank up fire to produce hot air and water. The last room is the calidarium: sheltered here are the remains of the two hot pools. From that on the left you may see the rests of the underground, through the collapsed floor. The flooring levels are in "opus spicatum", that is in bricks, herring-bone arranged; no traces are left of mosaics or frescoes. Returning to the Decumanus, and going along what once was an arcade with shops (tabernae), to the right you will find a flight of stairs which originally led to the upstairs flats; now there is a terrace which lets you have a very fine view of the town as well as the plan of the baths. It represents a quadriga with hippocampi abreast led by naked Neptune, holding a trident, and mythological sea creatures.

Descending from the terrace, you have access to the right to the arcaded courtyard, overlooked by service rooms. On the right corner there is a latrine; below there are ancient cisterns, now unreachable, built before the baths.

Terme di Nettuno

Mosaic of the Terme

Sabazéo, Via della Fullonica and Horrea on the Decumanus

Horrea of Hortensio

To the left, before the terrace, there is a short road, the Sabazéo, where you will find, few steps farther to the right, a badly preserved fence which is supposed to be either a Mithraeum or a Sabazéo (a place cult dedicated to Sabatius, a divinity from Frigia in Asia Minor, whose adepts practised orgiastic rites). Probably it dates from the middle of the III century. The inscription on a greyish-black background: "FRUCTUS SUIS INPENDIS CONSUMMAVIT" indicates the name of the devotee who donated the mosaic: "Fructus had it made at his own expenses".

On the Decumanus, to the right, there is the Caupona (= tavern) del Fortunato, named after the inscription on the floor dating back to the III century, FORTUNATUS (VINUM E CR) ATERA QUOD SITIS BIBE; it can be translated: "Fortunatus says: drink from the bowl to quench your thirst".

Turning to Via della Fontana, you will find to the left: the Insula of Ercole Bambino, the Insula with the painted ceiling with II c. AD frescoes, the Building of the Kilns, named after a big round kiln. Then turn right to find one of the most important Fullonicas (laundries) in Ostia. In the centre, there are three big pools with a slight slant of the floor for water drainage; to the right there are four small areas for the pressers of cloths - they were large embedded vases for clothes pressed by specific workers

View of Via della Fontana

with their feet. To the left there was a long counter with small ponds. The pillars in the centre let us suppose that the area had a roof. In the next area there was a small portico (note the position of the pillars) and on the left, in the corner, a sacellum with an altar.

Returning to the Decumanus, near the theatre, there is the so-called Christian

Sarcophagus in the Christian Oratory

Oratory, an ancient nymphaeum, symmetrical to that on the left of the theatre, which became a sacred place in the 4th and 5th century AD. According to tradition, St. Cyriacus and St. Aurea were killed here. To the first is dedicated a church probably built on the nymphaeum and his memory is preserved on the slab of the sarcophagus where you find written: HIC QUIRIACUS DORMIT IN PACE (here Cyriacus lies in peace); the church in the Borgo, at the exit of the excavations is dedicated to St Aurea. The Latin slab reminds us of the presence here of St. Monica, St. Augustine's mother (5th century).

On the Decumanus, to the left, are situated the Horrea, which are storage warehouses. They were located in axis with Via delle Corporazioni, which led to the river. They were built during the Republican age in the I century BC and are now 70-80 cm below the road level, due to the raising of the level of Ostia under Emperor Hadrian (117-138). The first warehouse - Horrea di Hortensio - is very striking for the inside inscription: it has a wide rectangular courtyard with magnificent tufa columns of the Tuscanic order. The second is the Horrea dell'Artemide, for such a statue found here; it does not present an arcaded courtyard, but has spaces directly overlooking the central area.

On the Decumanus, in front of the theatre are visible rests of the bases of a double arch dedicated by Caracalla (211-217) to the inhabitants of Ostia, as confirmed by some inscriptions in the warehouses.

Past the very few remains of a Republican Monument, you will get to a third warehouse "of the provisions" or "of the dolia" (=amphoras): it is a wide trapezoidal hall, where 100 jars for oil and wine have been found.

Jars in the Warehouse of the Doli

Bottoms of jars in the Warehouse of the Doli

the Theatre and the Forum delle Corporazioni

The Theatre from the Decumanus

Theatrical Mask

One of the first buildings to be excavated at the end of the 19th century was the Theatre, because its ruins emerged from the ground. Its present aspect refers to 1940 after the reconstruction by the archaeologist Calza and the architect Gismondi. The brick outer ring is completely "new", while the septa supporting the cavea date back to Augustus (end I century) - among them, they built shops arranged around the external arcade, or entrance ramps to the upstairs floors, barrel vaulted. Then, the typical feature of the Roman theatre is that the audience could have access below the tiers, while the cavea of the Greek theatre leant against a decline of the hill.

Take the central passage to get into the theatre: on the vault you may admire remains of elegant stucco decorations which suggest that it was a rich and refined place. The cavea is "complete", with tufa stairs: it is once more a reconstruction, made in occasion of the Universal Exhibition of Rome in 1942 (this event was never held, due to the war). In summers, performances are held here. In the side corridors (1), on either sides of the orchestra(2), you may see the walls of the first construction, dating back to the end of the I century BC, under the empire of Augustus, in opus quadratum and in opus reticulatum. At that time the theatre had two orders of

The cavea of the theatre

tiers and could accommodate 2,500 spectators. The place was enlarged under Commodus (180-193), then Septimius Severus and Caracalla (end of the II c., beginning of the III) with the building of one more order in the cavea (3) and of an upper gallery to seat 4,000 persons.

Most likely, in the 3rd and 4th century, water performances were held here: on the third step there are fragments of marble slabs set upright to let the flooding of the orchestra.

The proscenium (4) presents alternate semicircular and rectangular niches; the stage (5) was made of wooden boards laying on a sort of pool which was the iposcenium (the area situated below the stage), while the scene (6) was two-storey made. Fragments of marbles and masks are on the walls rebuilt laterally in opus quadratum. In the external wall to the right of the cavea (7), an upper big marble slab reminds the works of emperors Commodus, Septimius Severus and Caracalla.

Behind the scene of the theatre, extends the Forum delle Corporazioni, where the most important merchants and entrepreneurs of Ostia had their offices. The entrance was on the opposite side compared to where it is now, towards the Tiber: in the centre of the short side, in fact, the

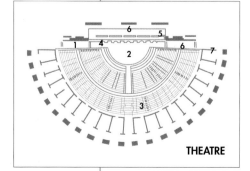

THEATRE

Piazzale delle Corporazioni

inscriptions are inverted in comparison with those of the other sides.

The complex arose in the first Augustan period (end of the I century BC), at the same time of the theatre, as witnessed by the lining up with its semicircle. Then, under Claudius (41-54) - who made also the new port to the north of Ostia - the arcade with brick columns was built; at the end of the II century the forum was restored and the whole square was raised of 40 cm. The mosaics in the halls of the corporations date back to this period - they are preserved only in part. If you walk along the area which was the ancient covered space, from right to left, you will note some figures with inscriptions inside the "stationes", the offices indicating the presence here of the trading corporations (only the most important ones are mentioned, marked by an asterisk):

-the tow and rope traders (stuppatores), very important in such a seaside town as Ostia;

- the tanners (PEL(liones));

- the sailors by wooden ships (NAVICULARIORUM LIGNARUM); worth a note is the mosaic with two ships towards the lighthouse;

- the corn traders symbolised by a man in tunic, who flattens that precious food in a bushel with scraper. It is not of high quality but it is interesting, because that tool was the symbol of those workers.

- the shipowners from Misa, east of Carthage in Tunisia, seen in the inscription NAVICULARI MISVENSES HIC;

- the shipowners from Musluvinium in Mauritania (NAVICULARI MV(S)LV(VIT)A(NI). Note the interesting cupid riding a dolphin and holding a whip.

- the shipowners from DIARRY(to), that is Hippo Diarritus, now Biserta in Tunisia;

- the traders from Sabrata (Libia), trading in ivory, represented by the elephant;

- the shipowners on their's own from Carthage, seen in the

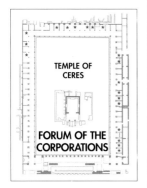

TEMPLE OF
CERES

FORUM OF THE
CORPORATIONS

inscription NAVICUL(ari) KARTHAG (iniensis) DE SUO;

- the shipowners TURRITANI (from Port Torres?) and KARALITANI (Cagliari) in Sardinia.

Then on the short side, you may see:

- an alive scene of loading amphoras from one ship to another;

- the representation of Nile;

Mosaic of a corporation

- various animals; these mosaics were at the entrance of the square;

- the inscription NARBONENSES indicating the seat of the traders from Narbo Martius in Gaul (France);

- the seat of the shipowners CURBITANI from Korba, in Tunisia.

Changing direction, on the second long side, note the numbers:

- with the inscription SOCOF , that is S(tatio) C(orporis) F(rumentorum) - the Corn traders;

- of the navicellarii from Alexandria (XANDRIN) in Egypt, where a great deal of corn was imported from;

- the seat of the CODICARI DE SUO, boatmen on their's own.

The last mosaics represent animal scenes: it was probably the first level of the square dating back to the first half of the I century.

In the centre of the Forum delle Corporazioni stands a Temple, dedicated to Ceres, according to tradition: it presents the typical Roman shape with a high podium, entrance stairs, pronaos (front portico) and one cella.

Ara dei Gemelli

In the south-west corner of the arcade stands the Sacello or Ara dei Gemelli: it is dedicated to the God Silvanus (ancient Italic god of nature and forests) and it is a chalk copy of a very refined altar with sculptures representing Romulus and Remus fed by a she-wolf on the bank of the river Tiber (below to the right); the edges are decorated with heads of bucranes (bulls skulls) with garlands, symbol of sacrifices. The original copy is in the Roman National Museum of Palazzo Massimo.

from the Domus di Apuleio to the Mithraeum delle Sette Sfere

Behind the Sacello is situated the so-called Domus di Apuleio, built towards the beginning of the II c. AD. The name comes from the inscription P.APULEIUS found on a lead pipe. Beyond a small atrium you would enter an arcaded courtyard with a basin in the centre; the rooms of the house were on the sides, some of them present valuable mosaics.

Domus di Apuleio

Returning to the Decumanus, after what remains of a semicircular nymphaeum of the beginning of the III c., symmetrical to that already mentioned, there is a wide area, just behind a colonnaded arcade: on the right you will find the remains of a small sacellum (= a sacred enclosure) dedicated to Jupiter, dating to the I c. AD, and soon after that a nymphaeum with three apses, dating from the middle of the II c. AD. In the back, standing on one podium, there were four small temples, with the same dimensions, front pronaos and almost squared cella. They referred to the late Republican period and are supposed to have been dedicated to the divinities Venus, Fortuna, Ceres and Hope. In the II-III c., a Mithraeum was built in the back - it was called mithraeum of the seven heavens or of the seven spheres, due to the floor mosaics which presented circle arches. It was dedicated to the cult of the Persian God Mithras (see the paragraph on the cults - p. 10-13). As almost all the mithraeums it has: a side gate to avoid indiscreet eyes, a small ritual well to the left of the entrance, two side podiums where the devotees kneeled or laid down and the altar at the far end. The seven semicircles correspond to the seven gates of heaven which the devotees had to pass through to reach their purification. Worth a note inside the first sphere is the sacrificial dagger with which Mithras had stabbed the bull to death. On the podiums six divinities (once they were seven) are represented, corresponding to the zodiacal symbols. The statues of Mithras' two genes, Cautes (day) and Cautopates (night) are on the side of the altar. The Collegial Temple stands on the Decumanus: it dates back to the II c. AD and is named after the inscription (reassembled on the opposite side of the road) which lets us suppose it belonged to the corporation of the builders.

Nymphaeum near the theatre

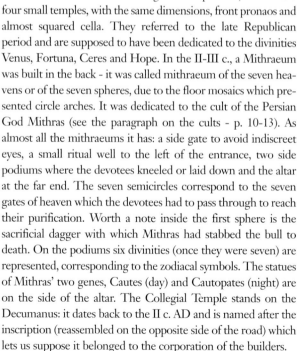

from the Seat of the Augustali to the Insula dell'Invidioso

G oing along the Decumanus you will find, to the
left, the seat of the Augustali (priests in charge
of the Emperor's cult). The building dates from the 150
AD and was then restored in the 3rd-4th c. The mosaics
found refer to this age, which demonstrates how the
Imperial cult persisted. Through a narrow and quite long
passage (to the left the remains of a column), you will find
an arcaded court on the right, a slightly raised altar if

Seat of the Augustali

compared to the hall, at the far end; the whole space was
covered with marbles, with two statues of Empresses,
Sabina (right) and Fausta (left) - the originals, now kept
in the Museum, have been replaced by casts. Here a great
statue probably of emperor Maxentius has been found
and moved inside. In the next room, there is a magnificent mosaic now covered with cupids holding a crown.
Coming back to the Decumanus, take Via del Mitreo dei
Serpenti to the left where the homonymous cult place is
situated. It is difficult to date it - probably the middle of
the III c. - but it has been built inside an edifice which
was restored many times. It is the simplest Mithraeum in
Ostia as it lacks of mosaics and stuccoes. The inside wall
paintings most likely refer to a previous cult place, similar to that of Pompei. On the sides of a Genius in white
tunic, shaded with yellow and red, and holding a crown
and cornucopia, there are two snakes: the male on the
back and the female on the left, symbol of evil and impu-
rity which Mithras always wins.
On the top there are the remains of a decoration with
flower garlands tied with ribbons.

Fresco in the Mithraeum dei Serpenti

Returning to the Decumanus,
past the Aula di Marte e Venere
(4th century), named after a statue now in the Roman National
Museum, you will find the Caseggiato del Sole (second half of the
II c.), on the left road. It is made
of 9 tabernae or shops lined on an
inner road and its name derives
from an inscription on plaster:
"The God Sun lives here". Probably this place was used for the
Sun cult, imported from the East.

Terme dell'Invidioso

Mosaic in the Insula dell'Invidioso

Well with amphoras

Farther on, on the Decumanus there are the big Horrea. It is a wide and complex building for the storage of goods (perhaps corn), built under emperor Claudius (41-54) and then restored by Commodus (180-192), who added a storey and introduced the suspensurae (small brick pillars under the floor to give air to the building), like all the thermal plants. It was arranged around a wide colonnaded courtyard and lined with narrow and long warehouses, all regularly located. Under Septimius Severus (193-211) the court was filled with other areas to enlarge it.

Past the few remains of a Republican temple to the right, take the Semìta (= side road) dei Cippi, the only road at Ostia we know the original name of; the complex of the Terme dell'Invidioso is situated to the left. They date from the I c. AD and include nice mosaics with sea subjects, undulated due to an earthquake. Worth noting is a hall, with two circular walls and ponds, seat of the frigidarium - a cold water swimming pool. On the road you will note a well made of stones and amphoras - it dates back to the 4th c. and its position lets us know that the road was not used in that period.

Opposite is the Insula dell'Invidioso, with shops lined on the road - the name derives from a fishing scene of the III c. with the inscription INBIDIOSOS.

from Via dei Molini to Via del Tempio di Diana

R eturning to the Decumanus - where you can
see the ancient level of Republican Ostia, 1
metre raised at the end of the I c. AD, you may take Via
dei Molini, continuing
the Sémita dei Cippi.
To the left, you can see
the walls in opus qua-
dratum of the ancient
Castrum (= fortified
town), dating from the
4th c. BC, when the
mouth of the Tiber was
to be fortified. Those
walls were then incorpo-
rated in some warehou-
ses of the II c AD. They
enclose a rectangular
space, intersected by the
Cardo and the Decuma-

Via dei Molini

nus, with four side entrances, according to the tradition
of the just founded Roman towns (see introduction
pages 8-9).
Farther on, to the left you will find one of the most
curious things in Ostia: the big Panificio (II century
AD) with shops where bread was sold, facing the road.
To the right of the main entrance note a slab representing a child with a cornucopia, symbol of abundance
while he feeds a snake; a symmetrical one to the left has
been lost.
In the back there were two halls with lavic millstones,
many of them still visible: they rotated thanks to a
donkey turning around and served for the production of
flour and pasta.
In the first room they crushed corn (the flour ran
between the two stones); in the second the flour was
kneaded and worked up. After having been baked, the
bread was sold in the fore shops. In the back there were
service rooms and a Sacellum dedicated to Sylvanus,
God of nature and forests, presenting pictures of the III
c. AD.
Going back, you should take the first road on the right,
Via di Diana, very well preserved for the presence here

Bakery, interior

Slab of the bakery

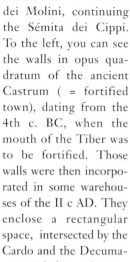

Caseggiato di Diana

MITHRAEUM

COURTYARD

CASEGGIATO DI DIANA

of some pavements. The first building to the right is the homonymous Caseggiato (second half of the II c. AD), named after a terracotta with the image of the Goddess. It is an extraordinary example of insula - a more storey building with shops lined on the road and mezzanines over them, with traces of corbels for the projecting balconies; it presented a central court, with fountain, the interior flats were arranged around it; the stairs were accessible directly from the road. Note, to the right of the entrance corridor, the latrine and, to the left, a hall with magnificent paintings of the mid II century.

In the north-east corner of the building, converted from two rather dark rooms, there is a Mithraeum (end of the II c. AD): as usual, the entrance to the first room is not in axis with the altar, to avoid indiscreet eyes; in the second room there are side brick benches, where the devotees knelt; traces of paintings are visible on the walls. In the back of the room, lit by a small loophole on the western wall, there is an altar with an oak carved in the front. It refers to the Republican age, but has been readapted, as says the inscription:

M. LOLLIANYS

CALLINICUS PATER

ARAM DEO DO DE

It refers to a certain Lollianus Callinicus, mithraic priest

Sign of the Thermopolium
with various food

bearing the title of pater, donating an altar to the God (DEO DO(num) DE(dit). A hole corresponds to the place where an oil lamp lighted the space during the rites.

Then in the back there is an aedicule with a niche characterised by small projecting pumice stones which remind us of the cave where Mithras was born; the arch was originally framed by two stucco semicolumns standing on travertine brackets.

Along the road, at the far end to the left, there is the famous Thermopolium, to sell food and hot drinks. It is very striking because it is intact - it was built in the III c. AD in a block of Hadrian's age (117-138). It presents three entrances with side seats and stone basins are still visible under the marble counter. Inside is situated a marble shelf with a wall painting about fruit, legumes, musical instruments and remains of amphoras buried in the ground.

The rear courtyard with fountain was furnished with tables to eat outside; the outside stairs led to a buried cellar. Almost opposite, to the right, is a big block with various insulae: that of Jupiter and Ganimede faces the road and has front tabernae, an internal court and paintings dating from the II c. AD.

The sight from the top is very striking.

Thermopolium, interior

from the Mithraeum di L. Menandro to the Caseggiato dei Doli

A s soon as you go out, returning to Via della Casa di Diana, take Via dei Balconi. At the far end, a stairway on the right leads you up to the Mithraeum of Lucrezio Menandro. It dates from the III c. and has been

The Museum

As a plaque says, it was founded in the middle of the 19th century in the Casone del Sale, a building dating from the 1400s and linked to the presence of salt marshes nearby. The present 12 rooms have been finished in 1977 by Doc. Valnea Scrinari, already Head of Excavations.

Room 1. Here are small boards some of which present magnificent scenes of everyday life. The most interesting ones are: counters for meat and vegetables, the scene of a birth. Other interesting pieces are - a fragment of a bronze pipe, a plan of a Roman temple and a chalk votive slab offered to the Goddess Bellona with footprints of a soldier that came back from war.

Room 2. Fragments of temple decorations dating back to the ancient castrum, with colouring traces.

Rooms 3-4. These are dedicated to Eastern religious cults flourishing at Ostia in the II and III c. AD. Starting from the back, you will find a beautiful statue of Mithras (II c.AD) slaying the bull, made by the Athenian artist Kriton, whose name is carved in the breast of the bull. Here is the simulation of the original space, with the window on the roof, where the Mithraeum delle Terme was located in Via della Foce. To the sides, heads of the two genes, Cautes, with sun rays (day) and Cautopates, with the moon (night). In the niche to the right there are 18 out of the 22 statues found in the Sanctuary of Attis near the Campo della Magna Mater.

Noteworthy are then:

- a pine tree with a snake coiled around (the God Attis wanted to be evirated for love and is supposed to have come back to life as a pine tree - see the paragraph about the cults);

- an altar with sculptures of 12 Gods from the I c. AD, coming from the sanctuary of Attis;

- a sarcophagus cover with a laying archigallus (follower of the cult of Cybele, Attis' lover) dating from the middle of the III c. AD;

- archigalli.

Room 5. It contains sculptures inspired by Greek art, among which a statue from an original Apollo of the 5th century. Note the whole weight on the tense leg, corresponding

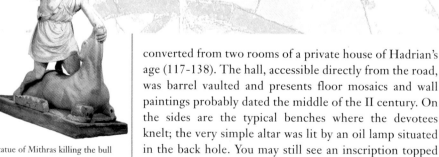

converted from two rooms of a private house of Hadrian's age (117-138). The hall, accessible directly from the road, was barrel vaulted and presents floor mosaics and wall paintings probably dated the middle of the II century. On the sides are the typical benches where the devotees knelt; the very simple altar was lit by an oil lamp situated in the back hole. You may still see an inscription topped

Statue of Mithras killing the bull

by a Crescent, a Mithraic symbol corresponding to the second level of initiation, and a dedication: to the invincible God Mithras by the slave Diocle in honor of Caius Lucretius Menandro, (priest of God as pater), a gift given to the God. Now we suggest that you visit the small but interesting Museum, also for the precious works here preserved.

Marble group of Cupid and Psyche

to the raised hip and the lowered shoulder, while on the side with the tense leg, the hip is lowered and the shoulder is raised: these art rules, seen also in other copies in the Museum, have been taken from Polycletus, an Athenian sculptor of the 5th c. BC - one of the best known in the classic age.

Room 6. It displays sculptures found in the Roman buildings, inspired by Greek art. In the centre of the room, there is a bust of wrestlers; on the sides - two Eros drawing their bows, inspired by the sculptor Lysippos (4th century) who conquered the third dimension - deepness; a magnificent portrait of Demosthenes, a Greek philosopher of the 4th c., and refined reliefs coming from the temple of Hercules in Via della Foce.

Room 7. It contains Roman sculptures inspired by Hellenistic works (III-I c. BC). The group of Cupid and Psyche is magnificent - it comes from the homonymous house; noteworthy is also a Perseus with the head of Medusa and the relief of the Graces.

Room 8. There are portraits of Roman emperors dating from the age up to Trajan (98-117). Note the nude portrait of Cartilus Poplicola without his head and arm (end of the I c. BC), whose tomb is situated outside the Porta Marina, on the Decumanus; a portrait of emperor Trajan; magnificent portraits of girls and boys with languishing eyes, full lips and chubby cheeks, dating from the end of the II c. AD; a very refined architectonic frieze, with geese, that, according to tradition, saved Rome from the siege of Gauls - it has been found near the basilica of the forum.

Room 9. Sarcophagi and sepulchral slabs of the II and III c are displayed here. Worth of interest is the sarcophagus found at Pianabella (near Ostia Antica train station, not far from the present cemetery) presenting scenes of Centauromachia inspired by Iliads (a battle between the man - symbol of intelligence- and the Centaur - symbol of nature).

Room 10. Sculptures dating from the II - IV century AD are preserved inside. Of great value is a statue in dark stone, inspired by Hellenistic works which perhaps decorated a temple dedicated to Isis (Goddess of Egyptian origin) in the town of Porto.

Room 11. In particular it is worth of interest an excellent mosaic in opus sectile found outside Porta Marina, dating back to the 4th - 5th century, with Christ Benedictory in the centre.

Going out the Museum and down some steps on the right, you find the Caseggiato dei Doli, an enclosure with big and charming "dolia" (terracotta jars), inserted in the ground, used for the storage of wine and oil. To the right you return to Via dei Dipinti and the Insula di Bacco Fanciullo, with paintings from the III c. AD and then go towards the Forum.

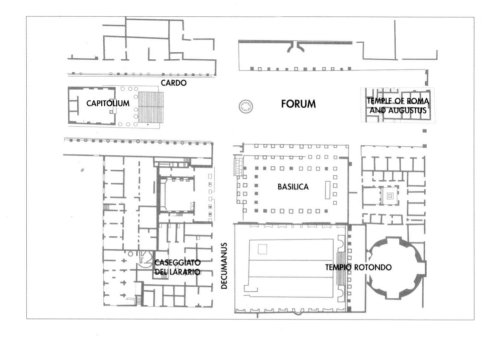

Traces of the Republican Temple

The Forum was the main "square" of the town; it was the place where the most important civic and religious buildings were situated. Usually it was rectangular, located at the junction of the Cardo and Decumanus or nearby. The forum of Ostia was built according to these rules.

Excavations have brought to light traces of a Temple of the Republican age (it is the rectangular area opposite the bigger temple). We have less news about the other buildings overlooking the square; the blocks in opus quadratum found below the "Curia" - probably the cella of an ancient cult building - belonged to this phase.

The area of the forum was radically transformed for the first time under Tiberius (14-37) when the temple dedicated to the Town of Rome and to the emperor Augustus was realised; the small round building of the Lares in the centre of the square dates a bit later on - it was consecrated to the imperial cult and you can still see some remains of it.

Other transformations occurred from the end of the I c. to the beginning of the II . AD with the building of the Basilica and the Curia. Then emperor Hadrian (117-

138) built the Capitolium, the biggest temple in Ostia and the side arcades with magnificent Corinthian columns. The Capitolium Temple was built in place of pre-existing buildings. It was dedicated to the Capitoline triad: Jupiter (father of all Gods), Juno (his wife, Goddess of fertility and protectress of

Capitolium

the Roman State) and Minerva (goddess of the town, of war and human activities).

A high flight of steps led up to the pronaos which had six front columns from the beginning; from here you entered the rectangular cella with three niches on each side.

It is supposed to be over 20 metres high and the walls in opus latericium presented an external marble facing - see the cramps of the holes. On the surface of the wall, note the rows of original yellow bricks, inserted to level and to give stability to the walls.

Capitolium, fragment of a cornice

Two side porticoes closed the northern part of the square. On the right of the area opposite the Campidoglio, over a rebuilt wall, they have reconstructed fragments of the cornice of the big temple, with dentils and ovoli of remarkable beauty.

On the south side of the Forum stands the Temple of Roma and Augusto, built by Tiberius in honor of the town and his predecessor. It is in axis with the opposite temple, but only the foundations survived. It was standing on a podium and had one cella with six front columns.

Statue of the Goddess Roma

Some fragments of the marble cornice, entablature and capitals - belonging to the back prospect - have been rebuilt in the left wall. The statue of the Goddess Roma, at the far end, was most likely located at the top of the pediment.

On the west side of the square there was the Basilica building from the I c. AD. In Roman towns this type of rectangular building with three or five aisles and

Reconstruction of the Temple of the Goddess Roma

Detail of the Temple of the Goddess Roma

entrance on the long side was used for the administration of justice.

In the remains you may see a double arcade towards the square and a central court. The very wide central area was the only nave and was paved with white and yellow marbles - the latter imported from North Africa (opus sectile). The podium of the judges was on the left.

Crossing the Decumanus, opposite the Basilica stands the so-called Curia. It dates from the I c. and was used for town council meetings. At Ostia the members of the council were 100 or 200, so the meetings could not be held in such a narrow place. For this reason the building is supposed to be a Republican temple, later rebuilt, with cella, pronaos and front columns.

Going behind the Campidoglio, along the Cardo towards the Tiber, there is an area built completely under Hadrian (117-138). In Roman times, this road was very important as it led from the Campidoglio to the river, which flowed parallel to the town - this fact is evident from the shops lined along it and the wideness of the road itself.

We suggest that you climb the two flights of stairs of the block at the far left end so that you will have a view of the bend of the Tiber and of the excavations. Turning left you will meet the block with corbel balconies and then the so-called block of the Corn Measurers, both dating from Hadrian's age.

Pass then to the Portico of the small market and to the Piccolo Mercato (middle of the I c. AD): they are two rectangular spaces with regular tabernae, now used for the preservation of ruins.

Area of the Forum view of the Tempio Rotondo

Returning to the forum and along the Decumanus towards the ancient shore, you will find to the left the Tempio Rotondo, a unique and interesting building dated the middle of the III c. AD (238-244), completed in the 4th c., not different, although smaller, than the Pantheon in Rome.

Like the famous Roman monument, the temple was preceded by a rectangular space and the altar was in the centre; a flight of steps led to the long and narrow pronaos; then the proper temple with alternate semicircular and rectangular niches in the walls - the latter even projecting outside; high columns on basements had to underline the circularity of the place, whose diameter was 18.30 m; the dome is also not supposed to be different from the more known Roman building.

On the sides of the entrance to the "rotonda" there were two spiral staircases (leading upstairs)

Spiral stairs of the Tempio Rotondo

only the first few steps survived. We do not know the function of the building (probably it was a pagan temple), but its relevance lies in the new type of architecture, typical of the late Roman period. Beyond a rectilinear space (the court), past a welcome area (the pronaos), suddenly the spectator found himself in a wide and "dynamic" space, made of straight and curve lines, certainly deriving also from eastern influence.

Tempio Rotondo, interior

Horrea Epagathiana

Caseggiato del Larario

The block of the Larario is a small market of Hadrian's age (117-138), with shops on the front road and ranged around an internal courtyard, with an aedicule made of red and yellow bricks probably dedicated to the Lares, divinities protectors of merchants.

Past what remains of the western Gate of the Castrum (4th c. BC), take Via Epagathiana to get to the homonymous Horrea - big warehouses ranged around a wide central court which belonged to the merchants Epagatus and Epafroditus, of Greek origin, as the inscription on a white marble says. The complex (middle of the II c. AD) is presently closed to the public because it is used for the safe keeping of the ruins found in the excavations - but it is still worth visiting from the outside for the magnificent clay gate, perfectly preserved. The portal is framed by two Corinthian semicolumns and, over the architrave, the tympanum presents particularly refined dentils and junctions. The second portal at the far end of the entrance corridor and the wall paintings in the spaces around the court, let us suppose that the Horrea were to house precious goods. The flats were upstairs, while the tabernae faced the road.

The Terme del Buticoso lie opposite: dating from the age of Trajan (98-117), renovated in the II c. AD, the Baths are named after a bare figure with an inscription below. Returning to the Decumanus, at the fork soon turn right. Take Via della Foce, at the beginning you will find remains of a Repu-

Tempio di Ercole

blican Sacello, to the right stands the Caseggiato del Mosaico di Porto, named after an important floor decoration representing the Portuense four-storey lighthouse with a flame on the top: unfortunately it is so badly preserved that it is quite impossible to read; it dates from the III century AD.

To the left is the Mithraeum delle Pareti Dipinte. Built into a domus of the II c. BC, then rebuilt in the I and II c. AD, it presents an oblique rear wall and the usual side podiums (with a small shelf for ritual objects). On the altar there is an inscription dedicated to the God Sun by a certain Sempronium. On the walls there are mithraic frescoes.

Tempio di Ercole, detail

To the right is situated a sacred area of the Republican period, adored up to the 5th c. AD. The most important temple is dedicated to Hercules. It dates from the end of the II - beginning of the I c. BC. It stands on a high basement and presented a pronaos with six front columns and one cella; it is supposed to be dedicated to Apollo for an inscription on the marble altar, in the centre of the pronaos. Most likely sailors and merchants gathered here to obtain the grace from the divinity for a good navigation. To the right lie the remains of another temple (end of the II c. BC), probably dedicated to Asclepius and Igea, divinities linked to the river Tiber. Opposite the temple of Hercules you may see traces of an imperial enclosure with four previous altars, particularly dear to the town.

Returning to the road, to the right you will find the

Mithraeum delle Pareti Dipinte, detail

Domus of Cupid and Psyche

Capitals of the Domus

Tempio dell'Ara Rotonda (end of the I c.), named after a circular altar found in it and now preserved in the Museum. Farther on, to the right, stands the Domus of Cupid and Psyche dating from the 4th century: it was one of the most elegant houses in Ostia. The atrium was paved with marble floors and facings and presented a nymphaeum with small composite columns; water flew from alternate rectangular and semicircular niches and was gathered in the wide basin.

Farther along Via della Foce, to the right stand the baths built by Hadrian (117-138), renovated at the end of the II century.

Absolutely not to miss is the suggestive Mithraeum delle Terme. It was built at the end of the II century in an underground corridor of the Terme, so as to be isolated and dark, like all the other places dedicated to this cult. The entrance, not in axis with the altar to avoid indiscreet eyes, led to a space, faintly lit by two skylights situated in the barrel vault: one was situated in the centre and the other at the southern end, so as to light the marble group representing Mithras in classical clothes about to kill the bull (it is a cast, the original is in the 3rd Room of the Museum). This remarkable oblique statue is signed on the breast of the animal by an Athenian artist - Kriton - and dates back to the II century. On the sides, there were brick benches with niches in the centre, no longer existing: here the devotees knelt. The vault and the back wall were stuccoed and painted - only few traces still survived.

Now you will visit the Caseggiato della Serapide, which was part of one grand complex, along with the Terme dei Sette Sapienti and the Caseggiato degli Aurighi and

Caseggiato del Serapide

was built under emperor Hadrian (117-138). The insula was ranged around a wide arcaded court, with huge pillars, lined with tabernae on the ground floor, unlinked with the road. A niche on the right-hand side houses a statue of Serapis. A still well preserved staircase to the left leads to a terrace overlooking the excavations; in ancient times it led to the upstairs flats which were accessible also through another way. Note the magnificent portal with side bucrans (= bull skulls bearing a sacrificial value) and traces of wall frescoes. Then you may see the contemporary Terme dei Sette Sapienti,

Terme dei Sette Sapienti, floor mosaic with tiger

built for the inhabitants of the two insulae. They are characterised by a big circular space, once domed, covered with a mosaic. The mosaic, dating from 130 AD, has been partly rebuilt with patterns which interrupt the pattern of the previous drawing, made of plants and achantus leaves getting bigger and bigger towards the external part so as to form an arabesque: inside there are figures of hunters and wild beasts. Inscriptions referred to the seven sages are preserved in a small area - among them Solon Atheniensis, Thales from Mileto, Chilon Spartan and some funny sentences alluding to bodily functions. The circular space was the frigidarium. The

Terme dei Sette Sapienti, floor mosaic with dog

Terme dei Sette Sapienti

wall paintings, among which a refined Venus coming out of the water, date from the first years of the third century, when the complex was restored.

The Caseggiato degli Aurighi (about 140 AD) is named after two frescoes situated in an internal corridor, which represent charioteers with crown and palm branch in their hands. The style is very synthetic with uniform colours,

Painting of the Aurighi

without shades and coloured outlines. It dates from the end of the II c. AD. Worth noting is also the court with high arcades almost reaching the second floor (the vaults were consolidated in 1963), the remains of remarkable frescoes on the walls and, outside, traces of balconies. It surely was a luxurious block, with wide and very decorated flats.

from the Casette-Tipo to the Sacello delle Tre Navate

C oming back to Via della Foce you will visit the ruins of the so-called Casette-Tipo. They were built during Trajan's times (98-117) and were named this way, since their discovery in the '30s, for their position in series, like our small deta-ched houses. Those flats were built for the entrepre-neurial middle class who was established in Ostia in the I-II c. AD, along with the development of the town of Porto. The external walls are in opus reticola-tum, those inside are in opus incertum. They were one-floor houses, with a mezzanine or terrace; each lodge was independent and specular to one another, both served by one stairway. The plan testifies how there was no waste and a lot of functionality.

Via della Foce

Returning to Via della Foce, pass to the right the Aula dei Mensores, seat of the cult of the corn measurers and the adjacent Horrea, all dating back to the beginning of the II c. AD and then you will find - to the right - the Terme della Trinacria. They are named after a mosaic which represents a head with three legs on top of each other -just two are now preserved - symbol of Sicily anciently called Trinacria; they were built in the first half of the II c., under the emperor Trajan and restored at the end of the same century.

Taking a path, after about 200 m., you will get to the so-called Imperial Palace: it is a great building dating back to the age of Antoninus Pius (138-161), restored at the end of the II century and characterised by magnificent arcaded courts decorated with stuccoes and frescoes. Noteworthy is the Mithraeum, situated on the right side of the com-plex: already dug in 1860, it is supposed to be dated during the age of emperor Commodus (180-192) who favoured the development of this oriental cult. It was narrow and

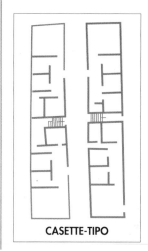

CASETTE-TIPO

Mosaic of the Caseggiato
di Bacco e Arianna

long with side benches, as usual, and is characterised by two alike inscriptions on the floor: SOLI INVICT MIT D D L AGRIUS CALENDIO (= Lucius Agrius Calendio gave a gift to the invincible Solar Mithras). Two small statues have been found here, representing Cautes (day) and Cautopates (night), dated 162 AD. It may be one of the most ancient mithraeums in Ostia.

Coming back towards Via della Foce and turning right, you will meet the Caseggiato di Bacco e Arianna dating from the middle of the II c. AD: it has magnificent floor mosaics which adorn the spaces to the right of an arcade facing a court. The decoration dates from 130 AD. In the smaller space there are squares with stylised naturalistic patterns, inspired by grapevine leaves, in which various cupids and birds are inserted, thus forming a particularly various and refined drawing. In the bigger space, inside a geometric frame there are still floral patterns inspired by grapevines, achantus and rose flowers which create different squares and circles. They enclose the battle between Eros and Pas (bottom) and Sileno (right), referee of the dispute, while Dyonisus and Arianna (sitting on a rock) and an old bearded man watch the scene. It symbolises the battle between intellectual love (Eros) and the animal one (Pan). The mosaic has been removed and cemented. Note the restoration: it consists of small black and white stones set continuing the original pattern.

Plaque with the inscription
JOVI SERAPI

Then there is an interesting temple dedicated to Serapis, a Greek-Egyptian divinity, whose cult was introduced to Rome at the beginning of the II century AD, and in use up to the 4th c., when it was forbidden by Christian authorities. As you can see, it is isolated from the rest of the town and we even know the date of its inauguration: 24th January 127, emperor Hadrian's birthday. The entrance gate to the road has, on the threshold, a mosaic representing the bull Apis, while the arcaded court is decorated with scenes representing animals and plants of evident Egyptian origin; to the right is a plaque which was probably on the pediment, with the inscription IOVI SERAPI (= to Jupiter Serapis) and this fact demonstrates how the cult was contaminated by the traditional paganism. The cella was

Temple of the Serapis with mosaic

situated over a podium accessible through a flight of stairs and was preceded by a pronaos with two front columns; it was rectangular and had an altar in the back.

Casts of Cautes and Cautopates in the Mithraeum della Planta Pedis

Farther on, to the right, there is the so-called Mithraeum della "Planta Pedis", named after a shoed footprint at the entrance. Probably it was dated the end of the II century and was converted into a museum in the 4th c. On the sides are the rests of the usual benches, while on the altar are casts with heads of Cautes and Cautopates.

Turning left, you pass to the Magazzino dei Doli where oil and wine jars are preserved half buried, and go to the Casa di Annio; going along the Cardo degli Aurighi, pass beyond the homonymous insula.

To the left, beyond a door obtained from a walled arch, there is the Sacello delle Tre Navate. We do not exactly know whether it was a mithraeum, because no objects connected to Mithras have been found here, but the position of the space with the two side podiums lets us suppose this. It presents Doric brick columns - just visible from outside; in the centre there is a small rectangular basin and at the far end, the altar. On the walls are rests of very ruined paintings, dating from the age of Hadrian (117-138). In the left space perhaps there was a kitchen for ritual banquets.

Planta Pedis

Taking the narrow road to the right, you will find, not far, a Calcara: during the Middle Ages, Ostia marbles were transformed into lime to build Roman civic buildings and churches.

from the Insula delle Muse to the Case Giardino

Insula delle Trifore

Insula delle Pareti Gialle

R eturning to the main road, to the right, you will meet the Insula delle Muse. It was built around 128 AD and was more luxurious than the Ostia block. The flats were all alike and got air and light from a wide square court; inside there were very beautiful wall frescoes. Unfortunately it is not open to the public.

It is adjacent, southwards, to the Insula del Graffito and the Insula delle Pareti Gialle - all dated the same. Opposite is the Insula delle Volte Dipinte, dating from the time of Hadrian, with magnificent frescoes on the walls and vaults - by now it is closed to the public. It was a three-storey building repainted in the 4th century.

Passing through the Thermopolium (cold and hot food shop), you arrive to the Insula delle Trifore (middle of the II c.). It is narrow and very long and is named after a series of three adjacent windows: it also presents traces of wall paintings.

Going again on the Decumanus, turning right soon, enter the splendid Domus del Ninfeo. It is one of the most beautiful and interesting private houses in Ostia. It was incorporated into a II c. building, the tabernae of which on the Decumanus Maximus have been left intact. It dates back to the 4th century, when the town began to decrease in population and very few wealthy men could afford to buy unused insulae and adapt them to

Domus of the Nymphaeum

their own needs. The narrow and long court is adorned by a nymphaeum with rectangular and semicircular niches. They alternate with small water falls pouring water, which was later gathered in a narrow and long basin, not centred, covered with spolia marbles.

It was overlooked by a slightly raised hall with a three-mullioned window and an entrance arcade leading to big halls and various small spaces, one of which apsed. The service rooms were beyond the court. Particularly worth of interest are the capitals of the columns which mark the entrance to the place: they belonged to the composite order and date later on, as you can see from the schematised achantus leaves and the smooth volutes of the 4th century. Noteworthy is also the floor of the place presenting geometric patterns made with various coloured marbles (=opus sectile). The capitals of the columns are restored of course. The Domus dei Dioscuri is nearby. Probably it is less suggestive than the previous one, due to the difficult analysis of the place and its bad preservation, but it is one of the biggest in Ostia. Also here an insula dating the II c. has been converted, in the 4th c., into a luxurious villa with the adding of an entrance, the transformation of rooms into a court, the restoration of the bedroom and the sitting room and for the presence of magnificent mosaics. The mosaic in the central space presents the Dioscuri, giving the name to the complex; that in the next room, Venus on a triton, surrounded by Nereids riding sea monsters. Beyond the big hall, to the left, lies a unique private thermal plant, the only one in an Ostia domus - it witnesses its anonymous owner's wealthiness.

Past the Domus dei Dioscuri, go farther on: you will be inside

Insulae

Case Giardino

Well of the Case Giardino

a unique area - the Case Giardino which were built, along with the following insulae, by emperor Hadrian (117-138), when the town was greatly restored and enlarged. Worth a note is this area to realise what the houses built for the high class were like - this fact is proved by the presence of numerous frescoes. They are the wealthier version of the already seen Casette- Tipo (see p.45): they were all alike, surrounded by a private garden, with two wide rooms overlooking the central rectangular space faced also by the smaller rooms. Internal stairs led to the upper floor or floors. The walls were frescoed with the typical yellow and red squares. In the communal garden, surrounded by other flats, there were square basins, while a very beautiful big arch gave entrance to the road parallel to the Cardo degli Aurighi: today this garden has been converted into a beautiful lawn.

from the Caseggiato della Fontana to the Synagogue

R eturning to the Decumanus, you will find to the left the Caseggiato della Fontana with an oil-lamp, dating from Hadrian's age. It is named after a beautiful fountain on the road with a seven-holed oil-lamp, where water poured out of. The portico, over the basin, arrived at the Caupona (tavern) di Alexander, named after an inscription on the floor (middle of the II c.). The erotic-grotesque paintings let us suppose it was a pleasure house.

Caseggiato della Fontana with oil lamp

To the right are the Terme Marittime dating from the age of Hadrian, restored later on and not visible yet.

Now you are at Porta Marina, one of the entrances to the town, far 1,200 m from Porta Romana. It is made up of one room with two external towers, and presents thicker walls than the others, to better protect the town from the sea attacks.

To the left lies the forum of Porta Marina, with a wide arcade court and apse at the far end, referring to the time of Hadrian, while to the right lies a burial Monument whose most ancient cubic block has been inserted in a Hadrian enclosure.

Soon behind stands the Domus Fulminata (second half of the I c., restored in the II and III) with its arcade court and fountain in the centre.

Crossing the road, there is the Sanctuary della Bona Dea, divinity of fertility, whose mystery cult was reserved only to women. The building (I century AD) was perhaps restored in the 4th.

To the left you will see the tomb of Cartilius Poplicola (I c. AD), very important to be preserved in the Hadrian restoration. The inscription, integrated by the restoration, reminds us of the career of the political man (eight

Caupona di Alexander

Terme of Porta Marina

times appointed duumvir and three times, censor), whose statue stands in the Museum. The fasces of the lictors divided into two parts with eight bends per side perhaps refer to his important office.

In the right side of the frieze you can see a ship ram and soldiers, probably referring to a defensive episode on the seashore.

A bit farther on, stands the baths of Porta Marina. They were begun by Trajan (98-117) on preexisting constructions of the I c. AD, completed in the middle of the II c. and restored at the beginning of the 6th c. Continue along the path.

You will arrive to the Synagogue.

This important place for the Hebraic cult is isolated from the other buildings, in the south-west area of the excavations. It proves the presence of a wealthy and numerous community in Ostia (see p.12).

(see p.12).

It was discovered in 1961 and it is one of the oldest in Italy and Europe, perhaps in the world, dating back to the middle of the I c. AD, restored in the 4th c. The walls in opus reticolatum belong to the first phase, while the parts in opus listatum to the second.

In ancient times it was on the side of Via Severiana, beside the shore (now where the road is).

Its position near the sea perhaps simplified the act of drawing water which used to feed the basin of puri-

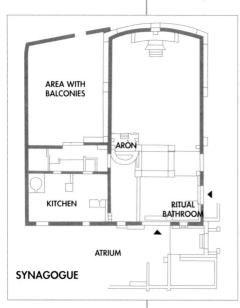

AREA WITH BALCONIES

ARÒN

KITCHEN

RITUAL BATHROOM

ATRIUM

SYNAGOGUE

fication. From Via Severiana you had access to an atrium with a small well, probably dated later; this area was open also on the side facing the shore, south-eastwards - it is supposed that there was another entrance.

In the main part there is the place for the ritual purification bath, had by men and women before their wedding; the place from where the women watched the ceremony; a place enclosed by four columns; the place for prayers with curve walls, and at the far end, the altar.

Probably the two columns on the sides of the altar formed, along with the other four, three naves.

In the apsed niche with two remarkable slender and small columns, topped by corbels with carved seven-winged candelabrums on, there was the Aròn, the sacred cabinet containing the scrolls of the Torah, (the law): it was directed towards the town of Jerusalem.

In the left rooms you will find: the kitchen with oven and a marble counter to prepare the azymous bread; past a corridor, it led to another bigger space with a bench leaning against the walls for the meetings of the community.

Detail of the corbel with candelabrum

from the Tabernae Finestrate to the Domus del Tempio Rotondo

Entrance of the Trajan Schola

Nymphaeum of the Trajan Schola

Returning to the Decumanus, past the building of the Tabernae Finestrate (II century), to the right you will see the Schola of Trajan, probably the seat of the naval smiths corporation. The II c. building had a wide arcade court in the centre with a fountain in the centre: in the back there was an apsed room with beautiful twisted columns. Opposite stood the Temple of the same corporation, with columns not yet used.

Soon after, on the same side there is the Christian Basilica. Between the end of the 4th and the beginning of the 5th c. this important cult place was constructed inside a building, once used as baths. According to someone, it was supposed to be the church of St. Peter and St. Paul - referred to by ancient texts; according to others, it could be possible to locate a small church (left) next to a baptistery (right).

Today you can see two narrow and long spaces, once separated by five columns: they preceded the two aisles ending with apses dug in niches.

On the two columns with Ionic capitals, leading to the left-hand side church, there is an architrave with an engraving: IN (Cristo) GEP, FISON, TIGRIS, EUFRA-TA, TI CR(st)IANORUM DUMITE FONTES, translated as follows: "In Christ, Geon, Fison, Tigri, Eufrate. Come close to the sources of the Christians". Note that the word Christ is made with the crismon, crossing of the Chi and the Ro, the first two letters of his name in Greek; note also that the above lines refer to the four rivers of Heaven, mentioned in the

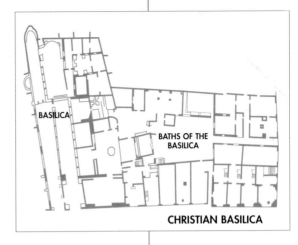

CHRISTIAN BASILICA

second book of the Genesis (confirming the hypothesis of the presence of a baptistery next to it). Moreover, some archaeologists think that the two letters "TI" are the abbreviation of TIGRINIANORUM (sect of the "Tigrinians"); others suppose it was an inadvertence of the builders, who re-used a slab already engraved.

From Vicolo del Dioniso, past two blocks, you will find, to the right, the Mithraeum delle Sette Porte: it was made in 160-170 AD from a I c. building, more restored later on. It presents the typical side podiums. The back wall was red, to recall the Sun and the fire: over it, there was a blue niche with a round arch. Over the podiums there are paintings with greenery and reeds of the III c. which remind us of the flowering of Nature by Mithras.

On the ground, near the entrance, lies a mosaic representing an architectonic pattern with seven arches supported by columns with classical capitals - the central arch is bigger than the others: they are the symbols of the seven levels of initiation before coming to true life. The central gate, more important, is that of the Sun. On the podiums there are still the symbols of Cautes and Cautopates and, in the back, a mosaic with a crater (symbol of water), a snake coming out of a rock (symbol of earth) and an eagle (symbol of air) holding a lightning (symbol of fire). Then, there is Jupiter holding a lightning and leaning on his sceptre and Saturn with a bearded and veiled face.

At the corner of Via della Foce and the Decumanus, on an atrium marked by majestic columns, there are the

Inscription of the Christian Basilica

Taberna of the fishermen

two famous Tabernae of the III c.: they had marble sale counters, very well preserved. The presence of basins and traces of ovens lets us suppose that also cooked fish were sold here.

An inscription INBIDE, CALCO TE (envious, I crush you) is near the dolphin, an animal disliked by fishermen, while snapping an octopus. In the back there was a meat-shop (macellum), overlooking a square, used as a market.

In Via di Iside stands the Temple dedicated to this Egyptian divinity. She was Osiris' wife, and was considered the protectress of sailors. Her cult was imported since the I c. AD, probably by Egyptian sailors who arrived at the mouths of the Tiber and had its most important moment on 5th March during the feast-day dedicated to the "navigium Isidis" (=Isis' ship).

From Via del Tempio Rotondo, you enter a second Collegial Temple of the II c., restored in the III. It probably belonged to the College of Tow makers. Later on, a Mithraeum was built inside. Then you get to the Domus del Tempio Rotondo, very badly preserved, dated from the II c., and renovated in the 3rd and 4th c. Around a court with basin there are various rooms: the main hall, slightly raised, with a three-mullioned opening. The whole house was paved with mosaics.

from the Forum Baths to the Caseggiato dei Triclini

Then you will arrive at the Forum Baths, the widest and most important complex in Ostia. They were situated in the heart of the town and were built, as it may be seen in the brick stamps and in the inscriptions, in different phases. The first, since 150 AD, was under the emperors Antonines, when the rooms of the main body were built and included the frigidarium (cold water pool), the perspiration rooms and the tepidarium (hot water pool); the second, under the emperors of the Severian dynasty (end II - beginning III c.) when restorations and addings were carried on; the third, since the 4th c. on, with the building of the curved wall of the frigidarium and the creation of the next Forum della Statua Eroica, and then the realisation of the rooms around the gymnasium with the characteristic late-ancient Ionic capitals. The entrance to the baths was on the west side of the Forum; thus, following a straight and symmetrical route, you had access to the frigidarium characterised by two side basins. Returning to the atrium, to the right there are very interesting places of different shape, each with a different function, all southwards directed so as to have light but above all sun heat through wide windows during the afternoon - when most of the people crowded the baths. The place was octagonal in shape, perhaps it was a heliocaminus (=room facing the sunlight to have benefits in winters). From here, through a narrow passage, you could enter the original and dynamic elliptical room, perhaps used as a laconicum (= perspiration room); you may still see the terracotta pipes on the walls, inserted between the wall and the marble facing (they were used to heat the room with air coming from the underground areas

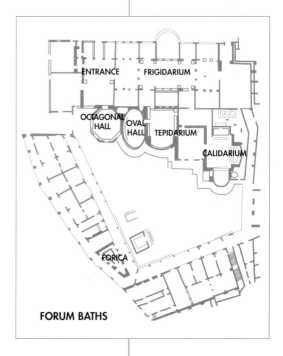

FORUM BATHS

Forum Baths - oval

Pipes

Forum Baths

where boilers were located), and the side benches which stressed the particular shape of the room, once dome covered. Then there are other spaces, heated by terracotta pipes, perhaps used as tepidaria (= warm water pools). In the first space there are two rectangular pillars with composite capitals; in the second there are two magnificent reconstructed Corinthian columns. The space was then a calidarium (hot water pool) with three basins fed by two boilers located behind the left hand side pool, now inaccessible. A narrow and long corridor led to an open colonnaded trapezoidal space with some areas for body activities. This is one of the most suggestive places in ancient Ostia: with a bit of imagination you may rebuild the original south prospect of the Forum Baths. Even the latrines are interesting to see, along with a small temple, without dedication, overlooking the square.

Wide underground spaces have been discovered in the baths and they served to heat the whole area, and, towards the "semita dei cippi", a cistern has been found which was filled with water conveyed from the underground to the surface - this was done through a wheel of about 10 m. diameter.

Now take Via della Forica: here you may see a public latrine, built at the end of the 4th century inside two existing shops. Farther on, there is the Forum della Statua Eroica, built later on pre-existing ruins dated II c. AD - it is an arcaded square almost squared-shaped. It is named after a male statue situated in the centre. From the Decumanus you may enter the Caseggiato dei Triclini (II c. AD), named after the presence here of benches on the three sides of rectangular areas.

Forica

from the Domus del Cardo to the Campo della Magna Mater

Then return to the Cardo Maximus, and past the Forica, you will see the Domus di Giove Fulminatore. It dates from the II c. AD and is named after a slab with a dedication in Greek to Jupiter throwing thunderbolts. It was remodelled in the 4th century. The plan is always the same: rooms ranged around a central court with impluvium. The back wall with niches was built later. Then there is the house with a niche covered with mosaic of the I c. BC with two courts: the first presents a basin, the second, a well - the mosaic niche dates from the II century.

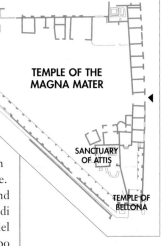

The Nymphaeum degli Eroti (4th century) is well preserved - it is a small square area, marble covered with three niches on the sides and a square basin in the centre. Past the Domus delle Colonne, the Domus dei Pesci and the Caupona del Pavone, you will find the Caseggiato di Ercole, with remains of selling counters, and the Terme del Faro. Then you will get to a wide open area, called Campo della Magna Mater (Roman divinity corresponding to the oriental Cybele, Goddess of fertility) which is a very interesting sacred complex. The structure of the sanctuary dates from the second century AD: it is a triangular square, whose longer side, adjacent to the walls of the town, was made of an arcade with brick columns; the north-east side was lined with tabernae facing the road; the north-west side ended with the Terme del Faro and the Mithraeum degli Animali. At the vertex of the triangle, towards Porta Laurentina, there are some small temples dedicated to oriental cults. The most important and accessible is the Sanctuary of God Attis, God-shepherd of Frigia, who was compelled by Cybele to evirate for love, according to the legend. The sanctuary is made of an almost square fence, with basin in the centre, slightly below the square level, overlooked by a small rectangular cella with apse and side niches; the entrance is flanked by two telamones (= columns, statue-shaped), located on a basement and representing the God Pan: inside there is the reproduction of the statue of Attis - the original is in the Museum Lateranenses. In the same vertex of the triangle there are then

Sanctuary of Attis

Square of the Campo della Magna Mater

other two unidentified fences, the Temple of the Schola degli Astiferi (spear carriers, perhaps ritual dancers) and, in the corner towards the walls, the temple of Bellona: an ancient Latin divinity linked to war, perhaps identified with the goddess Ma, venerated in Asia Minor. This last temple, built in the first half of the II century AD, then restored, is made of a long trapezoidal court, faced by a temple made of an atrium with two front columns and a rectangular cella.

On the opposite vertex, near the external road, the Temple of Cybele is situated - Cybele was the oriental goddess of fertility, linked to Attis. The building, dating from the II century was built like the typical Roman pagan temples. Through a staircase you got to a basement where a cella preceded by a pronaos or atrium with possibly four front columns was situated. The devotees could not go inside and then the rites had to be held outside, where traces of the altar may still be seen.

To the left of the sanctuary stands the Mithraeum degli Animali. Originally it was isolated from the Campo della Magna Mater; its entrance was to the west and, unlike all the other buildings used for this cult, it did not present the side podiums. It dates from the II century but unfortunately it is badly preserved. It is perhaps related to the temples of Attis and Cybele, oriental divinities from Frigia. The floor mosaic is very interesting as you may distinguish starting from what it is supposed to be the altar:
- a naked man with frizzed hair holding a sickle and shovel for fire;
- a cock, an animal announcing the rise of the day with a crow or an owl, one of the levels of the cult initiation;
.- a scorpion, symbol of destruction as it is able to attack the bull's testicles;
- an undulated snake; according to the Mithraic tradition it drank the blood of the bull, beaten by the scorpion;
- a bull head with the knife that was used to kill it.

Temple of Bellona

from the Domus di Medusa to Via degli Augustali

The Domus di Medusa (III century AD) over-
looks Piazza dei Gorgoni; it is ranged around
a very small trapezoidal court and presents irregular
rooms. Some rooms host
mosaics with Gorgon's heads
- a mythological figure with
serpent-like hair and open
wings. According to tradition, this divinity was also
called Medusa and her
looks turned any beholder
to stone; she will be killed
by Perseus.

Domus of the Fortuna Annonaria

Past the Molino, there is
the beautiful Domus del
Protiro (4th century),
built on a pre-existing
structure. Its restoration
ended in 1990. An entran-
ce with columns, topped by an elegant triangular tympanum, leads to a corridor, beyond which there is a
court preceded by a nymphaeum.
The main hall had a three-mullioned window and a
floor mosaic. Below the villa there was a wide cistern.
We suggest that you climb the stairs to appreciate how
it was planned.
Past the Terme del Filosofo, turn to Via della Fortuna
Annonaria, where the homonymous Domus is situated:
it has been built inside a two-storey block of the II century AD and originally presented various shops on the
road-front. During the 4th century it was converted
into a wealthy residence, with an internal court. The
name derives from a statue situated in the garden, on
the right. Past the vestibule, marked by a protyrum, you
entered an arcaded garden on three sides.

Entrance to the Domus
of the Protyrum

To the right of this garden, separated by a step, there
was the main hall, characterised by a semicircular apse
with niches at the far end, and a nymphaeum with a long
rectangular basin to the left. Note the interesting columns
with composite styled capitals, topped by a dosseret
(trapezoidal block between the capital and the arch, used
a lot in Byzantine architecture to lighten the arcades).

Mithraeum del Felicissimo

They witness the loss of the formal classical values, typical of the 4th and 5th century AD, when the Western Roman Empire begins to fall. To the left, there was a big space paved with a mosaic.

The following domus, improperly called Caseggiato dei Lottatori, perhaps because the building was the seat of the homonymous college during the Imperial age, dates from the III century AD.

Past the entrance, you enter a court with a central basin and other various spaces - the main one presents remarkable mosaics, dark on white background.

On the same road, to the right, there is the Mithraeum del Felicissimo.

It dates from the second half of the III c. AD and presents the typical plan of this kind of cult buildings: a long space with side benches, whose access is not in axis with the altar to avoid indiscreet eyes. But this mithraeum is interesting above all for the floor mosaic with the symbols of the different levels of initiation. Starting from the entrance, you will find:

- a crater (symbol of water), an altar with fire, two pilei (= conic hats) of the Dioscuri which represent the sky. Then in the various squares there are:

1. a crow, a small ritual vase and a caduceus (rod with two snakes), symbol of Mercury; 2. oil-lamp and diadem, symbol of Venus; 3. Knapsack, helmet and spear, symbols of the soldiers protected by Mars; 4. fire shovel,

Mosaic in the Mithraeum del Felicissimo, detail

lighting and sistrum (musical instrument) to symbolise Jupiter; 5. an arched sword, sickle with star and crescent to point out the protection under this celestial body; 6. solar crown, torch and whip for the quadriga to point the sun; 7. plate, magic wand, helmet and arched sword to represent Saturn.

Then, a wide ritual vase with ears of corn and small flowered branches, symbolising the world created by Mithras and the

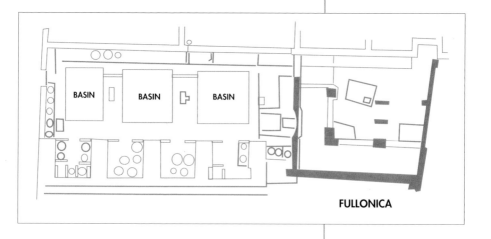

FULLONICA

inscription FELICISSIMUS EX VOTO F(ecit) - Felicissimus made it as ex-voto.

Turning left to Via degli Augustali you will see a Fullonica, an ancient laundry. It has a wide rectangular space with brick pillars in the centre; among them there are four basins for cloth washing and dyeing: they date from the middle of the II century AD, but restored: note the still visible water pipes and, on the right, near the wall in opus reticolatum, the remains of the "suspensurae" (bricks one on top of the other) where hot water passed through towards the basins.

Small wooden beams were inserted among the pillars to hang up the washed or dyed clothes. On the three sides there were almost completely underground vases, strictly connected for the saltus follonicus, where special workers, jumping and treading, washed the clothes. Near the forth side, to the left, there were small brick basins and benches. We do not know whether the central part was covered; the pillars have been raised (from the rut on the brick wall) and the modern shelter protects the fragments.

Then return to the Decumanus until Porta Romana. Before going out, watch the Necropolis.

A vase in the Fullonica

Necropolis

Via delle Tombe

A s soon as you go out, you will find the Necropolis to the right. The first archaeological excavations were carried on in the middle of the 19th century, then researches continued between 1910 and 1920. The Roman necropolis (from Greek = towns of the dead) was located outside the town centres, for hygienic reasons, along the main roads. The tombs in Via Appia dating from Ancient Rome are famous. In Ostia there are necropolis along Via Ostiense, Via Laurentina (outside the homonymous entrance gate) and along Via Severiana towards Porto.

Two tomb monuments have been found on the Decumanus, soon after Porta Marina, seawards. No traces have been found of the 4th century Ostia; we suppose that the external necropolis has been covered by the edifices of the Imperial Age.

It is very difficult to date the tombs situated along Via Ostiense, because sometimes they are made of previously used materials. Most of them date back to the I century AD, when cremation was in use: the ashes were put inside small vases and located in the columbaria. Since the II century burial in tombs spread over. Via dei Sepolcri, parallel to Via Ostiense, dates from the II century AD, when the necropolis extended beyond the main road. The tombs were inside fences, usually uncovered and the walls were plastered.

Note the following four tombs, among the most interesting ones. Taking Via Ostiense, to the right, towards

Tomb of the Archetti

Porta Romana, you will visit the II century AD tomb of Fabricius Fabius Hermogenes: it presents a marble slab on the cubic sepulchre with the name, almost illegible.

Taking the path to the right, towards Via dei Sepolcri, you will see, in particular:

- the tomb of the small arches (first half of the I century AD), with inside columbaria and the original entrance opposite respect to where it is now (you get into it through a narrow path); the front part presents six brick pilasters framing the five openings.

Detail of the inscription MHN

The upper arcades are decorated each with a different pattern, but with yellow and red brick alternate with grey pumice stone. Those walls were then plastered; after the restoration the tomb faced Via dei Sepolcri. Here you will still see an architrave with the letters MHN engraved on it; they have to be added, on the right and on the left, respectively with the letters H and S, thus forming the abbreviated sentence: H(oc) M(onumentum) H(aedes) N(on) S(equetur) = the heirs will not have this monument.

- The tomb of the Colombari Gemelli, so-called for the symmetry of the two side spaces. It dates from about 50 AD. Here too, the entrance was northwards so in the internal road overlooked by a beautiful brick façade. Two small stairs led upstairs, while in the centre, in Via dei Sepolcri, there was the place for cremation.

Colombari Gemelli

- The tomb of the Ovii. It is adjacent and slightly later than the previous one. It is hypogean, partly underground, barrel-vaulted and presents counters with funeral urns on three sides. The inscriptions let us suppose that it belonged to the Oviis.

the Borgo of Ostia Antica

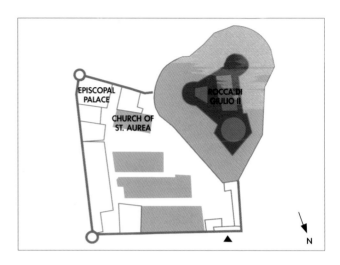

This small area is a precious example of Renaissance architecture, preserved through times, and dates from the 4th century, when numerous Christian churches were built along the seashores, partly over Roman buildings.

The Church of St Aurea became important soon - in fact Ostia became seat of the bishopric in 313 and the bishop had important functions, among these to crown the pope.

For almost unknown reasons, the Diocesi of Ostia was joined to that of Velletri in 1150, but it did not lose its central importance. In the following centuries, some bishops of Ostia became popes.

During the Middle Ages, Ostia maintained a remarkable economic function for the presence here of salt marshes (see p.3). Along with the Arabian conquest of Sicily (827), Pope Gregory IV decided to have Ostia fortified with a small town, named after him - Gregoriopoli: it may be located near the bend of the Tiber, where the Renaissance village will flourish.

After the Avignone exile of the 14th century, which caused a total abandonment of the town, pope Gregory XI (1370-78), while coming back to Ostia from that French town, found that the fortified village was scarsely populated.

Later on, Martino V (1417-31) built a new round

Entrance to the Borgo

defence tower, which still characterises the place.

Other enlargements of the small area were carried on by Cardinal Guglielmo D'Estoutville, bishop of Ostia from 1461 to 1483, who aimed to become Pope. He built the three rows of terraced houses and restored the walls, adding his numerous insignia.

Terraced houses in the Borgo

The fortification of the Tiber mouth reached its apex from 1483 to '86, when Cardinal Giuliano della Rovere - then Pope Giulio II - built a citadel and a church around the tower of Martino V. The architect is supposed to be Baccio Pontelli from Florence. The triangular fortress has two round towers and a pentagonal rampart towards the river and, thanks to the plain ground, it was supposed to defend the whole area. It is an interesting example of military architecture of the so-called period of transition, when new fire arms were introduced and used together with the traditional Middle Age arms (crossbows and bombards).

After some decades, in 1557, an important event for the history of the village occurred here: during a November night, due to a very strong flood, the Tiber changed its course, erasing the so-called Ostia bend, beside where the citadel had been built. Thus the fortress lost its proper function, as it was situated 1.5 km far from the river.

Door and windows of a house

In that period there was a degradation of the whole Ostia area, nonewithstanding the presence of some suburban villas owned by famous noble families, such as the Chigi and Rospiglioni.

The Village decayed and went to ruin; the houses were used as stalls and barns.

The area became a marsh and was reclaimed since the end of the 19th century; in 1884 the Pope called for 500 farmers from Romagna, led by Nullo Baldini. They organised a co-operative society, one of the first in Italy and began to drain the area, conveying the waters in still working canals, which served to flow the waters. A plaque on the wall of the Village, on the side of the main road, reminds us of that important page of history.

Home entrance

Church of St. Aurea

Insignia of Cardinal Della Rovere

Slab of St. Aurea

The church was built over a paleochristian pre-existing structure; it has one nave and is dedicated to the Ostian martyr St. Aurea, who was martyred nearby.

It was begun by Cardinal d'Estouteville and completed by Cardinal Giuliano della Rovere in the first years of his office; the numerous coat of arms on the façade represent the durmast topped by a cardinal hat. The bell-tower and the Sacristy date from the first twenty years of the 16th century. The materials used are very elegant: the structural parts, such as the parastades on the plinths, the cornices, the gate, the entablature and the mouldings of the tympanum are in travertine; the parts used for filling are brick-made. There are some Gothic elements: the two-mullioned windows and the rose window on the façade. On the top of the tympanum note the acorn, fruit of the durmast tree, which completes the building.

The interior is simple and harmonious; it presents a truffed roof with the d'Estouteville's coat of arms. The paintings in the apse date from the 16th century; the Candelabrum is made of ancient pieces. To the right there is a chapel with two walled plaques: the first is a fragment of a slab reminding us of the death in Ostia of St. Monica, St Augustine's mother (408); the second is a cast of a plaque with the inscription CHRYSE (the Greek name of Aurea), perhaps in honor of the woman Saint buried nearby.

the Episcopal Palace

Episcopal Palace

I n some rooms of the Episcopal Palace - the residence of the Bishop - there are interesting frescoes, already mentioned by Giorgio Vasari in 1568 and discovered in 1977 by the then parish priest Geremia Sangiorgi.

Those frescoes have been attributed to the painter and architect from Siena Baldassare Peruzzi (1481-36), helped by Cesare da Sesto, pupil of Leonardo da Vinci e Domenico Beccafumi. For a long time they have been neglected, because the rooms were converted into a lazareto in the 17th century, and the walls were painted white. Heraldic coats of arms bearing the name of the client are on the architraves of the doors and the windows, and also on the edges of the paintings: they belong to Cardinal Raffaele Riario, pope Giulio II's nephew and appointed bishop of Ostia in 1511. He restored the old building behind the church, enlarging the complex towards the church of St. Aurea.

The inscription R/EPS/OSTIE/CAR/S. GEO/SRE/CAMER points out that Riario was also Cardinal of St. George and Camerario of the St. Roman Church. The paintings have squares that alternate with pilasters decorated with the classical pattern of the candelabrum. The monochrome scenes simulate ancient reliefs inspired by the Trajan's column in Rome. Probably there is some propaganda: as the Roman emperor submitted the Daci-living in Romania, considered as barbarians and foreigners, as the papal army would have defeated the foreign army of the French King Louis XIII. Noteworthy is the scene, not represented on the column, of the funerals of emperor Trajan, attributed to the mannerist painter Beccafumi.

the Rocca of Giulio II

T he first core of the citadel was built under pope Martino V Colonna (1417-31), when the building activity flourished again in Rome and the sea-

shores were fortified, after almost a century of neglect, due to the Avignone schism.

It was the high tower, now still visible above the defensive walls, which pope Pius II Piccolomini defined "excelsam et rotundam" in his Commentarii (1461). It was a three-storey building and 22.30 m high. Its diameter measured 14 m and

The Fortress

contained in the lower level, an oven and a mill that are now half underground, yet visible. According to some hypotheses, it was supposed to be the forth vertex of the quadrangular village which previously had three cylindrical embattled towers.

Cardinal Giuliano della Rovere (Bishop of Ostia from 1483 to 1503, the same year in which he was appointed pope as Giulio II) realised the impressive fortress, probably following a plan by the architect Baccio Pontelli from Florence.

The fortress has a triangular plan and three keeps at the vertex: two are circular and directed towards the town; one is pentagonal and has the tower of Martino V incorporated: it faces the river - the place where the heaviest attacks could come from.

The ravelin

The fortress marks an important period in the history of military architecture in Italy. In fact, along with the typical elements of the Middle Ages fortifications, such as the embrasures, used to throw arrows and boiling oil and the ravelin - a fortification at the entrance of the fortress, for the first time, there are suitable instruments of defence against fire arms, introduced to Italy in the second half of 1500s. The main new structures are:

1) cylindrical and pentagonal keeps, whose forms are made in such a way that the new iron bullets have less chances to hit perpendicularly the surfaces, instead tending to bounce - as they arrive diagonally;

2) a moat with scarp (the oblique wall at the base of the construction) along the whole perimeter of the fortress;

3) two "cut" towers, less vulnerable against iron balls and a terrace letting the soldiers move more quickly;

4) "large merlons" which are a better form of defense from the new arms (the visible merlons are an error of restoration by the architect Italo Gismondi in the '40s);

5) casemates - rooms situated at the bottom, along the whole perimeter- to shoot grazing shots.

Tower of Martino V and pentagonal rampart

Now enter the hexagonal ravelin, not in axis with the proper entrance; it was a sort of independent fortress, with merlons and casemates. You will be opposite a magnificent Renaissance portal, with the inscription:

IUL(ianus) SAONENSIS EPISC(opus)
CARDINALIS OSTIENSIS FUNDAVIT
BACCIO PONTELLO FLORENT ARCHITECTO

South bastion of the Fortress

The sentence (Cardinal Giuliano di Savona, bishop of Ostia founded (the fortress) thanks to Baccio Pontelli, architect from Florence) has been studied a lot, because it confirms the attribution of this work to the Tuscan artist.

Inside the threshold you will read:

CUSTOS FIDE, CAVETO DOLIS
SPES IN ARCE: SOVITO METUM

which can be translated as: Faithful custodian, beware of deceptions, hope is in the fortress, free yourself from fear.

Then enter a trapezoidal court, where you will find

Sign of the Fortress

some Roman sarcophagi from the near excavations of Ostia, a well with the coat of arms of Cardinal Giuliano della Rovere and numerous stone balls, left over from the 16th century battles. On the walls you may still see traces of the preparation of the wall for the frescoes which had to cover all the surface of the court, now completely lost.

From the court, through a door on the right bearing the insignia of Cardinal Giuliano, known as Pope Giulio II (1503-1513), you enter the papal apartments, through a flight of stairs, also reachable while riding horses.

The paintings on the vaults are attributed to the school of Baldassarre Peruzzi (a refined painter from Siena of the 16th century). The insignia at the entrance of the apartment and those on the fireplace belong to Pope Paolo III Farnese (1534-49).

Continuing along the stairs, you will get to the terraced floor, from where you have a beautiful sight of the village.

Walking along the pentagonal rampart you may admire the coat of arms on the keep, towards the place where once the Tiber flowed (the present road); you may read the marble slab below it.

To the right: coat of arms of Martino V Colonna (1417-31); from left to right: coats of arms of Sisto IV (1471-1484), Innocenzo VIII (1484-1492) and Giulio II (1503-1513).

This fact indicates that the building of the fortress was begun by Martino V, continued by Innocenzo VIII and

Sisto IV and completed by Giulio II. Most likely, the coat of arms of Giulio II had the cardinal hat, then replaced by the papal one.

Coming back, past the trapezoidal court and a unique spiral stairs, you will arrive at a corridor with some casemates, which surrounds the fortress. Those small rooms were used for grazing shots; they have a long hexagonal plan and are barrel vaulted: they are one of the features of the fortress of Ostia. In the same corridor, high openings let

Fortress of Giulio II

light and air in during the time of war.

At the base of the keep there are still visible traces of the ancient oven, the second in the fortress, protected by thick walls. Worth noting inside the south-east rampart (directed towards the church) is the presence of a circular space with concentric steps and vault covered: it was the papal bathroom.

This stresses the importance of the fortress, as both the pope and the cardinal wanted to have all the available facilities to spend even very long periods there. According to some historians, the above said bathroom had something in common with the "calidaria" of the Roman baths - in fact Ostia offered numerous and clear reference models, also at the end of the 15th century.

As already said, in 1557 the fortress lost its function as a defence for the city of Rome, due to the changing of the course of the Tiber.

In 1567 the tower of St. Michele was built, probably on a design by Michelangelo thus moving away the customs functions. In 1612 Paolo II had the canal on the right-hand side of the mouth of the Tiber re-opened (the ancient Trajanian pit); for those reasons Ostia decayed completely. Few inhabitants remained inside the fortress - they worked in the salt marshes and fished in the pond.

In the middle of the 19th century the fortress was converted into a prison by Pope Pius XI; after the war it was restored by architect Italo Gismondi who made it appear more "mediaeval" adding the merlons.

BUILDING TECHNIQUES

OPUS QUADRATUM: IT REFERS TO A MASONRY OF LARGE TUFA OR STONE PARALLELEPIPEDAL BLOCKS, IN HORIZONTAL ROWS.
THE BLOCKS OFTEN MEASURED A MULTIPLE OF THE ROMAN FOOT (29,6 CM).
IN THE ARCHAIC AGE (8TH-7TH C. BC) THEY WERE JUST ONE ON TOP OF THE OTHER; IT MEANS THAT THEY WERE BUILT WITHOUT MORTAR, BEARING THEIR OWN WEIGHT; LATER ON, THE BLOCKS WERE HELD BY IRON OR BRONZE CRAMPS, WITH VERY LITTLE BINDER TO JOIN THEM. FOR EXAMPLE AT OSTIA: CASTRUM WALLS (IV CENTURY BC) AND SULLAN WALLS (I CENTURY BC) WHICH SURROUND THE TOWN.

OPUS CAEMENTICIUM: IT REFERS TO A MIXTURE OF : A) LIME (CRUSHED CALCAREOUS STONE), B) SAND OR POZZOLANA (VOLCANIC EARTH), C) PIECES OF STONE, BRICKS, MARBLE OR TRAVERTINE. ALL WAS MIXED WITH WATER AND POURED IN WOODEN FORMWORKS. ONCE SOLID, THE FORMWORK WAS TAKEN AWAY.
IT WAS VERY RESISTANT AND WAS LARGELY USED SINCE THE III CENTURY BC IN THE INTERNAL WALLS, SO AS TO HAVE CURVED LINES IN PLANS OR IN VAULTS OR DOMES.
IN DIFFERENT AGES, THE OPUS WAS COVERED IN DIFFERENT WAYS, AS ILLUSTRATED HERE BELOW.

OPUS INCERTUM: IT IS THE MOST ANCIENT COVERING OF THE OPUS CAEMENTICIUM.
IT IS MADE UP OF PYRAMIDAL TUFA BLOCKS, WITH IRREGULAR BASES, SET IN THE MORTAR, SHOWING THE LARGEST PART.
THE WALL WAS THEN PLASTERED. IT WAS USED FROM THE II C. BC TO THE I C. AD.
AT OSTIA AN EXAMPLE CAN BE SEEN IN THE NORTH WALL OF THE DOMUS OF GIOVE FULMINATORE.

OPUS QUASI RETICULATUM: IT REFERS TO SMALL TUFA BLOCKS SET IN QUITE REGULAR ROWS, EVEN IF NOT PERFECTLY ORGANISED. USED FROM THE END OF THE II C. BC AND THE BEGINNING OF THE I C. AD.
AT OSTIA: WALLS DATING FROM SULLA'S AGE (BEGINNING OF THE I CENTURY) WHICH SURROUND THE TOWN.

OPUS RETICULATUM: COVERING MADE OF PYRAMIDAL TUFA BLOCKS WITH SQUARE BASES: THE TOP IS SET IN THE MORTAR, WHILE THE BASE IS EXTERNAL, THUS MAKING A CHARACTERISTIC NETWORK PATTERN WITH OBLIQUE LINES AT 45°.
THE EDGES WERE MADE OF RECTANGULAR TUFA BLOCKS, ONE ON TOP OF THE OTHER, THE WALL WAS THEN PLASTERED.
THE OPUS RETICOLATUM WAS USED FROM THE

FIRST HALF OF THE I C. AD TO THE END OF THE I C. AD, WHEN IT WAS GRADUALLY REPLACED BY THE OPUS MIXTUM.

OPUS LATERICIUM: FROM LATERES = TILES OR SUN-BAKED BRICKS: PRESSED AND FLATTENED CLAY WITH OR WITHOUT STRAW, SUN-BAKED (MATTONE CRUDO). USED BY PEOPLE IN MESOPOTAMIA, IT WAS THEN USED BY THE ROMANS FROM THE II C. BC TO THE AGE OF AUGUSTUS (BEGINNING I C. AD), WHEN THE KILN-BAKED BRICK WAS INTRODUCED.

OPUS TESTACEUM: OR TESTACEA STRUCTURA: COVERING OF THE OPUS CAEMENTICIUM MADE OF BAKED BRICKS; TRIANGLE SHAPED, THE BRICKS HAD THE VERTEX IN THE MORTAR AND THE HYPOTENUSE IS EXTERNAL.
SOMETIMES THESE WALLS WERE LEFT IN SIGHT, AS IN MODERN TIMES; OTHER TIMES THEY PRESENTED REGULAR HOLES WITH THE CRAMPS OF THE MARBLE COVERING DRIVEN IN.
THEY WERE RARELY PLASTERED. THE OPUS TESTACEUM WAS USED DURING THE AGE OF AUGUSTUS (BEGINNING OF I CENTURY ANNO DOMINI) AND IT WAS GRADUALLY REPLACED BY THE OPUS VITTATUM.

OPUS MIXTUM COVERING OF THE OPUS CAEMENTICIUM, MADE OF THE OPUS RETICOLATUM AND THE OPUS LATERICIUM. THIS MASONRY WAS USED IN THE EDGES, SO AS TO STRENGTHEN THE SIDE WALL AND CONTRASTING THE POSSIBLE CRACKS ALONG THE OBLIQUE LINES. VERY USED DURING THE FLAVIANS (FROM 70 AD), UNDER TRAJAN (98-117) AND HADRIAN (117-138). THE WALL WAS THEN PLASTERED.

OPUS LISTATUM OR VITTATUM: FROM VITTA =BEND. COVERING OF THE OPUS CAEMENTICIUM FORMED BY ALTERNATE HORIZONTAL ROWS OF BRICKS AND PARALLELEPIPEDAL SMALL BLOCKS OF TUFA; SOMETIMES THERE ARE TWO ROWS OF BRICKS AND ONE OF TUFA.
THIS OPUS WAS VERY REGULAR AND WAS USED SINCE ANTONINUS PIUS (138-161); IT BECAME PREDOMINATING SINCE THE 4TH C. AD, ABOVE ALL UNDER EMPERORS MAXENTIUS (306-12) AND CONSTANTINE (306-337), PROBABLY DUE TO THE POOR PRODUCTION OF BRICKS. THE WALL WAS THEN PLASTERED.

BRICKSTAMPS: FACTORY MARKS ON TILES OR BRICKS. OFTEN, WHEN THE BRICK HAS NOT BEEN RE-USED, IT CAN DATE THE BUILDING. USED FROM THE I CENTURY BC TO THE AGE OF CARACALLA (198-217).

RAMPART: embankment inside a structural wall, polygonal in shape at the angular vertexes of the fortress, used for a further defence.

CARDO: in the Roman town, it refers to one of the two main streets, directed North-South.

CASEMATE: a small and often hexagonal space, at the foot of the fortification, used for cannon or rifle shooting, at man-high (=grazing shot). The etymos is uncertain; probably it derives from "armed house" or "mad house", in relation to the heavy noise made by the explosions, or from "house of Mars", god of war.

CASTRUM: originally, it was a Roman military camp, rectangular in shape, planned with two main roads crossing at right angle: the Cardo and the Decumanus. At their intersection there was the Forum - the main square surrounded by temples and public buildings. Generally speaking, this term refers to Republican towns founded according to this plan. For example Pavia, Florence, Ostia.

CAUPONA: tavern.

CELLA: in the ancient Greek and Roman temples, it was a particular space with statues of divinities in and was forbidden to prayers.

CRISMON: Christian symbol deriving from the first two letters of the Greek word Christós.

DECUMANUS: in the Roman town, it was the second axis, perpendicular to the cardo and with a direction from East to West.

DOMUS: it is a patrician Roman house, characterised by one or two various courtyards, overlooked by the rooms.

FULLONICA: it is a laundry for washing and dyeing clothes. The Romans used the urine to whiten clothes - it was put in proper basins or in big terracotta vases.

HORREA: they were warehouses used for food storage.

INSULA: more storey-house, with shops on the street level.

PILASTER: a decorative semicolumn, engaged in a wall and projecting only slightly from it.

NYMPHAEUM: monumental fountain.

ORDER OF ARCHITECTURE: In architecture it refers to the column and its entablature. According to the historians of the Renaissance, there were five orders:

1-DORIC: it developed in the 7th century Before Crist in the Greek region of Peloponneso and Magna Grecia; the column was fluted and without a base; the capital had a flat abacus (upper part) resting on the echinus (lower); above it, the entablature was made up of a flat architrave, a frieze with grooved elements (triglyphs) and carved slabs (metopes); a cornice completed the whole.

2-IONIC: developed in Asia Minor and in the Attic region since the 6th c. Before Crist; the Romans made a

great use of it. The column with a base was taller and slenderer; the capital had symmetrical volutes; the entablature had a three-levelled architrave and a frieze showing a continuous relief.

3-*CORINTHIAN*: Greek in origin (5th century BC), the Romans developed it; similar to the Ionic order as far as regards the column and its entablature, the capital had acanthus leaves.

4-*TUSCAN*: used by the Etruscans since the 6th century BC and by the Romans, it simplified the Doric order - the column was not fluted and had a base.

5-*COMPOSITE*: used by the Romans since the end of the I century AD; the capital had Ionic volutes (in the upper part) and acanthus leaves in the lower part. The entablature is similar to that in the Corinthian order.

PARASTA: a structural flat pilaster, engaged in a wall and projecting only slightly from it.

PRONAOS: in the Greek and Roman temples, it referred to an open space in front of the cella.

PROTYRUM: it was a small atrium with columns, arch and/or tympanum, showing the front entrance to a house or a church.

DOSSERET: architectonic element, typical of the late-ancient period. It topped the capital in order to slender the column and the above arch.

RESTORATION: It is used to preserve ancient finds through times. In Ostia, these restorations brought to the partial completing of the walls. They used the same building technique, but caused 1 cm back completing and the covering of the same walls was made with brick concrete to let water better flow.

RAVELIN: (from Latin "revellere" = to detach); it refers to the small fortification, built to defend the main entrance to the fortress. It was separated from the walls, which consisted in merlons, embrasures and casemates.

SCARP: it is an oblique wall at the base of the fortress, which served to deviate fire shots better than straight walls could do.

SUSPENSURAE: piles of bricks on which the floors of the baths (to heat the rooms) or those of the warehouses (to ventilate food stockage) laid on.

TABERNAE: shops, also for handcraft activities.

THERMOPOLIUM: it was a tavern where cold or hot food and drinks were sold to public.

Contents

List of planimetries

BIBLIOGRAPHY

E. ROCCHI, Le fonti storiche dell'architettura militare, Roma 1908.

G. TOMASSETTI, La Campagna romana antica, medioevale e moderna, Roma 1910.

D. VAGLIERI, Ostia, Cenni storici e guida, Roma 1914.

G. LUGLI - G. FILIBECK, Il Porto di Roma imperiale e l'agro portuense, Roma 1935.

G. CALZA - G. BECATTI - I. GISMONDI - G. DE ANGELIS D'OSSAT - H. BLOCH ed altri, Scavi di Ostia, voll. I -X, Roma 1953 /79.

C. CALZA, Una grandiosa impresa archeologica. La rinascita di Ostia Antica, Roma 1941.

M. FLORIANI SQUARCIAPINO - R. CALZA, Le necropoli. Scavi di Ostia, vol. III, Roma 1962.

M. FLORIANI SQUARCIAPINO, I culti orientali ad Ostia, Leiden 1962.

AA.VV., Mysteria Mithrae, (atti del seminario marzo 1978 a cura di U. BIANCHI), Roma 1979.

S. DANESI SQUARZINA - G. BORGHINI (edited by), Il Borgo di Ostia da Sisto IV a Giulio II, Il Quattrocento a Roma e nel Lazio, catalogo della mostra, Roma 1981.

P. TESTINI, Archeologia cristiana, Roma 1980.

C. PAVOLINI, Ostia, Bari 1983.

C. PAVOLINI, La vita quotidiana a Ostia, Bari 1991.

M. A. RICCIARDI - V. S. M. SCRINARI (edited by), La Civiltà dell'Acqua in Ostia Antica, voll. I e II, Roma 1996.

© Copyright 2000
Ats Italia Editrice srl
This volume was edited by
ATS Italia Editrice - Roma
Via Francesco Sivori, 6 - tel. and fax 0639726079 - 0639726080
www.atsitaliaeditrice.it

Author
Sonia Gallico
Editing and Technical Coordination
Frida Giannini
Graphic Project
Ats Italia Editrice (Roberta Belli)
Cartographies
Ats Italia Editrice (Sabrina Moroni)
Photolitography
Scriba - Florence
Printing
Papergraf - Padua
Photographs
Archives ATS Italia Editrice (G. Bocchieri - F. Borra - M. Cirilli - G. Cozzi)
Archives Scala
Translation
Tiziana Vallocchia

ISBN 88-87654-21-2

The editor is available for those having rights on the unfound iconographical sources